Divine Justice, Divine Judgment

D1350922

FACETS

Selected Titles in the Facets Series

Darwin and Intelligent Design
Francisco J. Ayala

The Care of the Earth
Joseph Sittler

*Christian Faith and Religious Diversity:
Mobilization for the Human Family*
John B. Cobb Jr., editor

God: A Brief History
Paul E. Capetz

Islam: What Non-Muslims Should Know
John Kaltner

The Measure of a Man
Martin Luther King Jr.

*Religion and Empire: People, Power,
and the Life of the Spirit*
Richard A. Horsley

Technology and Human Becoming
Philip Hefner

Who Is Christ for Us?
Dietrich Bonhoeffer

Divine Justice, Divine Judgment
Rethinking the Judgment of Nations

Dan O. Via

Fortress Press
Minneapolis

DIVINE JUSTICE, DIVINE JUDGMENT
Rethinking the Judgment of Nations

Cover photo © James Nachtwey / VII Photo.

Library of Congress Cataloging-in-Publication Data

Via, Dan Otto, 1928–
    Divine justice, divine judgment : rethinking the judgment
of nations / Dan O. Via.
        p. cm.
    ISBN 978-0-8006-3896-2 (alk. paper)
    1. Christianity and politics.   2. Christianity and justice.
3. Judgment of God.   4. Social justice—Religious aspects—
Christianity.   I. Title.
    BR115.P7V46 2007
    231.7'6—dc22

                                                    2006038919

Manufactured in the U.S.A.
11   10   09   08   07   1   2   3   4   5   6   7   8   9   10

Contents

Preface
vii

Part One
Theological Perspective:
Justice, Judgment, and Evil

1. Introduction: Justice, Judgment, and
National Repentance
1

2. Distributive and Retributive Justice in the
Bible and in Aristotle
11

3. The People under Judgment: A Biblical Motif
27

4. 9/11 as an Evil Committed by al-Qaeda
35

5. 9/11 and Justice in America:
A Hermeneutics of Judgment
60

Part Two
What Have We Been Doing?
Where Might We Be Healed?

6. Introduction: In Between Warning
and Disaster
83

7. What Have We Been Doing Since 9/11?
Domestic Affairs
86

8. What Have We Been Doing Since 9/11?
Foreign Affairs
115

9. Conclusion: Dangerous Scenarios
and Hopeful Opportunities
149

Notes
183

Preface

Most of my previous work in theological ethics has been in New Testament ethics. My focus has been on the New Testament texts themselves in light of their formal literary features, their historical contexts, and other critical considerations, seeking to determine what the texts meant in their original contexts. I also believe that a hermeneutical concern about contemporary meaning and relevance has an inherent place in biblical interpretation.

In the present work, however, I am rather using the Bible for Christian ethics. In my use of the Bible I will be critically rigorous, but my focus and emphasis are different from previous work in New Testament ethics. I focus on contemporary problems and draw on the Bible, and on other sources, in order to understand those problems and to set forth norms and justifications. I speak of the Bible rather than just the New Testament because the subject matter has elicited as much—or more—

attention to the Hebrew Scriptures/Old Testament as to the New Testament.

That subject matter is the biblical understanding of history and social justice as the criterion for assessing any society. I seek to examine American domestic and foreign policy and to interpret recent American history. There are many very good things about the United States of America; my task in this book, however, is not to extol its virtues but rather to look critically at some very troubling policies and actions. This task for me is both a necessity and a source of sadness.

I want to thank Michael West and Neil Elliott of Fortress Press for their help and encouragement and my good friends George Telford and Charlotte McDaniel for their critical readings of all or parts of the manuscript. And without the computer skills, discerning eye, and unflagging support of my wife, Margaret, this work would not have seen the light of day.

Dan O. Via

PART ONE
Theological Perspective:
Justice, Judgment, and Evil

1.

Introduction: Justice, Judgment, and National Repentance

The purpose of this book is to explore the tensive and conflictive relationship between the biblical understanding of justice and contemporary American social, economic, and political practice. I argue that, assessed in light of the criterion of biblical justice, many American practices begin to look like injustice. At last, however, I also want to consider some possible forms of national repentance that could reduce the disparity between biblical justice and American injustice.

My task requires a consideration of the topic of judgment because there is in the Old Testament an unbreakable connection between justice and well-being, on the one hand, and between injustice and disaster—judgment—on the other.

To examine justice and injustice in abstraction from the issue of judgment would be to rupture an integrated biblical construct. Given the national jeopardy associated with judgment in the Old Testament, however, and given the anxious sense of threat in the U. S. since 9/11, we cannot address the theme of judgment without raising the question how it might be related to the events of that distressing day. That question can hardly be escaped in light of the magnitude of the event and the way that it has been interpreted by the Bush administration and perceived and assimilated in the American collective consciousness.

The theological theme of judgment in history is complicated and controversial, and it will be understood and evaluated in very different ways. Furthermore, its rightful place in today's theological understanding has been compromised by the use to which it has been put by the Christian right. Therefore, I want to make very clear, here at the beginning, how I will develop this idea (see also Chapter 5 on "A Hermeneutics of Judgment").

Scholars use the term *hermeneutics* to describe a philosophical or theological procedure that inquires into how we understand the literary, historical, and social phenomena of life. Whenever we interpret a text or an event, we do so from a certain standpoint, an angle of vision or a question to which we seek an answer, whether or not we do so consciously. There is no disinterested interpretation, so the most objective interpreter is not the one who claims to be disinterested but the one who is most aware and critical of his or her angle of vision, the position from which he or she interprets.

We can understand and interpret something new and perplexing by seeing it in terms of something older and more familiar. Understanding moves from the old to the new so that the new becomes comprehensible. In the case before us, the new, perplexing thing is 9/11; the familiar lens through which I will be looking in order to see it aright is the centuries-old prophetic understanding of the operation of justice and judgment in human history (Chapters 2 and 3).

When we see the new—9/11—as prophetic judgment, we have to be critically aware that the new is not exactly like the old. We want to avoid the vicious circle of simply imposing the old on the new so that our understanding ends just where it started. We must see the new as the old in order to have access to the new at all, but at the same time, we have to take account of the new by making ourselves aware of its defining differences from the old. And we have to give arguments to show why, despite the presence of the different and unprecedented in the new phenomenon that we want to understand, the old still offers a clue to its meaning.

Social injustice in ancient Israel brought judgment. If we recognize that American social injustice is quite similar, can we—should we—regard 9/11 as divine judgment? The events of 9/11 and their concomitants are so complex and labyrinthine that I cannot answer that question with an unqualified "yes." But I believe that one can make a plausible, tentative—but dialectical—case that 9/11 can and should be understood as divine judgment upon America.

That thesis will raise immediate protests. On what biblical and theological grounds, by what hermeneutical moves, might one say such a thing? Does this effort put me in the camp with Jerry Falwell and his cohorts? (After the 9/11 attacks,

Falwell made the public claim that feminists, homosexuals, and abortion-rights advocates had provoked God to lift America's curtain of divine protection; the groups he named "helped this happen." Falwell later apologized.)

My answer is that I accept the prophetic understanding of God's judging action in history as a hermeneutical lens that is still valid for Christian theology. I vigorously reject the specific way in which Falwell applied the theme of judgment, however, and I regard the "family values" underlying his assertion as disvalues. I have a very different view than he does about the most serious deformity in America's soul.

In the pages that follow, I propose that a theological interpretation of 9/11 can understand it paradoxically as both an injustice, an evil, inflicted upon the U.S. (Chapter 4) and also as a judgment against us for our violations of justice (Chapter 5). My hope in raising these issues is that even if, at some future time, our nation must respond again to events that we experience as evil, we will have made such changes that we shall not have reason to interpret that evil as judgment against us.

Falwell's language about God's "lifting the curtain of divine protection" presumes that heretofore America had had a special, protected relationship with God. I reject the myth of American exceptionalism implicit in his language, according to which God has chosen us to have a privileged place among nations. Others have suggested that to hold a nation subject to divine judgment, or to call a nation to repentance, presupposes that the nation has a covenant with God that has been violated. Since the U.S. has no such covenant that would be comparable to biblical Israel's covenant, this objection continues, it is theologically inappropriate to say that we Americans are subject to God's judgment and should repent. This view, however, misses an important Old Testament principle, one that is central to my position throughout. Significant Old Testament texts, none more notable than Amos 1–2, make it unmistakably clear that *all* nations are accountable to God's demand for justice. Knowledge of that demand and of the nature of justice is available to *all* human beings as such. Those that violate the demand are subject to judgment.

It is also true, however, that for the Old Testament there is no wholly uncovenanted nation. In the story of Noah, God enters into an eternal covenant with all humankind (Gen. 9:9, 16, 19). In the covenant text itself, God makes an absolute commitment to humankind without imposing any conditions on the human partner (Gen. 8:21-22; 9:11, 15). In the ensuing narrative, however, human beings are held culpable for their offenses (9:22-25); indeed, in Gen. 11:1-9 the whole human creation, descended from Noah, is held accountable for its arrogance and is punished. From this biblical point of view, no nation—even a secular nation—is beyond accountability to God and the responsibility to repent.

Others have objected that it is not possible for a *nation* to repent. But, of course, nations *can* repent. The basic meaning of repentance in the Bible is "to turn" or "to change." By the repentance of America, I mean a turn or change from relative injustice to a more expansive and inclusive justice. Nations can do that. As John Rawls has convincingly argued, in

a secular democracy justice is a political phenomenon, enacted by the representatives of the people.
Rawls believes it is possible for national societies
to move to greater expressions of justice (although
he does not think America is presently inclined to
do so). But if *national* repentance means turning
to a fairer enactment of justice through the democratic political process, on what possible grounds
could one suggest that a nation *cannot* do that? In
fact our nation did so, strikingly, in the 1930s with
the New Deal, and in the 1960s with civil rights
and voter rights legislation.

My proposal to interpret 9/11 as divine judgment is not an unqualified assertion but a flexible,
circumspect response. The events of 9/11 were
extremely complex, both politically and theologically, and no interpretation is beyond doubt. In
the end, when I ask if 9/11 was a judgment against
America, I answer with a dialectical "yes" and
"no," but leaning toward "yes."

A final problem has to do with the nature of
the event of judgment itself. Here again, my hermeneutical lens is provided by the prophets of
ancient Israel. The issue hangs on two points.

1. The first is the relationship between God and
the event of judgment in history. When the prophets
speak of events of judgment, whether in the past or
anticipated in the future, they seem to regard these
events as invasive incursions or penetrations by
God into the normal course of human history: "I
will tell you what I will do to my vineyard. . . . I will
make it a waste" (Isa. 5:5-6); "I will appoint over
[the people] four kinds of destroyers. . . . I will make
them a horror to all the kingdoms of the earth" (Jer.
15:3-4); "Now the end is upon you. . . . Disaster

after disaster! See, it comes" (Ezek. 7:3, 5); "I will come against the wayward people to punish them" (Hos. 10:10); "Therefore the tumult of war shall rise against your people" (Hos. 10:14); "I gave you cleanness of teeth in all your cities. . . . And I also withheld the rain from you. . . . I struck you with blight and mildew" (Amos 4:6, 7, 9).

We get a rather different picture in Isa. 10:5-13, however. Again we have God devastating a godless Judah by means of a human instrument: a personified Assyria. But here Isaiah also reflects on the nature of the coming judgment. God initiates it and carries it through, but Assyria is not a passive, manipulated puppet. Assyria has no consciousness or intention of being God's agent for punishing Judah. To the contrary: that nation acts out of its own aggressive, imperialistic goals, and attributes its success to its own wisdom and strength. We have in this text, then, the view that God succeeds in carrying out God's purposes by acting through—not by negating—the agency of semi-autonomous human beings. God's action is not an invasion from a transcendent "elsewhere" that breaks into the historical sequence but a hidden, immanent power that works within the historical dynamics of international relations. (By the term *immanent* here I do not mean the abstract philosophical claim that God is *in* everything, but rather make the more historical theological claim that God can choose to *be active* anywhere.)

I take the dramatic, electric language the prophets use to proclaim divine intervention as an invasive action from above as metaphor. The biblical writings often regard puzzling, troubling, frightening historical events, especially disasters, as direct divine acts. One thing (the event) is seen as something other (God's act), creating a semantic tension. In this moment of perception, the sudden event becomes both like and not like an intervention. This allows us to perceive God's hidden action as present in it, but this does not require that God is acting directly from a transcendent beyond; rather we can still recognize that the event is generated by human interests and purposes. Speaking of divine intervention functions to focalize the particularity of the event and to underscore its divine dimension, to express God's intention to hold the people accountable and to issue Israel a wake-up call about a possibly devastating threat.

I will explore this important Old Testament motif, of God's power working as a hidden factor in the human enterprise without nullifying human freedom or subverting the integrity of human actors further in Chapter 3. One of its implications is that consequences flow intrinsically and organically from human acts. In the Old Testament this applies both to individuals and to the nation; and while this movement proceeds immanently on the horizontal plane of human activity, the Bible presents God, as creator of the human world, as somehow its author and director.

Isaiah can also describe judgment without speaking of an invasion by an external force, but as the culmination of a process of internal social disintegration. (Isaiah does not put the picture together in a systematic way, but the elements are there.) God is the source of an event of judgment (3:1), but *as the hidden, immanent director who actualizes the consequence that proceeds from a complex of human actions.* The *complex of human actions* is the perpetration of social injustice that creates divisions among people—specifically, between rich and poor (Isa.1:23; 3:14-15; 5:8, 23; 32:9-14)—and the *consequence*, that is, the divine judgment, is the explosion of these divisions into chaotic anarchy (3:1-15).

2. The second point concerns the relationship between the prophet and the event of judgment. The *event* is quite objective, of course, as a historical occurrence (we know, for example, from non-biblical sources that Assyria invaded Judah in the eighth century B.C.E.). But such an event is not "objectively" a divine judgment—it could also be accounted for, in the normal course of history, in terms of national ambitions and motives—but *becomes* a moment of divine judgment through the prophet's interpretation. The event's meaning existed not in itself but in the prophetic word.

In sum, for the prophets, divine judgment is an event that occurs in the course of the normal push and shove of human history, but is interpreted by the prophets as an action of God to hold the people accountable and to punish them. We need not understand the event as an intervention of God "from above," but we can see it as an occurrence in which the hidden, secret activity of God comes to specific and concrete expression within the dynamics of human history.

In the following pages, I use this prophetic understanding of judgment as a vantage point for asking whether 9/11 should be understood as an act of divine judgment. Does this imply that God *willed* or *intended* the events of 9/11? Absolutely not. As in the case of Assyria in Isaiah 10, the actions of the terrorists grew out of their own freedom and semi-autonomy, and were motivated by their own religious and political goals. But from the prophetic vantage point, that fact does not mean that the event could not become the occurrence of judgment.

In the long run, the most important implication for us of the prophetic understanding of judgment is that it regards the climactic event as preceded by signs—namely, the phenomena of divisive injustice in society—that can be discerned, actively addressed, and possibly overcome.

If we, as church and as nation, are unable to recognize and act upon these signs already at work in our nation and world, we will have failed to answer two of the most important theological questions of our day. Some fifteen years ago, Jack Forstman raised these questions in his incisive book *Christian Faith in Dark Times*. Our present time is much darker than the time in which he wrote, and the questions are that much more pressing: (1) Does the Christian faith contain understandings of God, self, and world that will enable us to recognize demonic evil before it becomes firmly entrenched among us? (2) Does the Christian faith enable the courage to name the demonic publicly and say "No" to it?[1] The demonic in our own time, I contend, is represented not just by the rise of terrorism, but by our government's excessive, foolish, and militaristic reaction to it, which threatens the well-being of the world and the character of America as a free society.

2.

Distributive and Retributive Justice in the Bible and in Aristotle

Aristotle (384–322 B.C.E.) and the Bible differ significantly in their understandings of justice, but comparing them can sharpen our perception of both of them. Aristotle's formal categories have been a major contribution to the Western comprehension of justice.[1] We can frame the discussion in terms of these categories without imposing Aristotle on the Old Testament.

Aristotle

For Aristotle, justice is concerned with human relationships. Among the virtues, it is the only one that is for the good of others, because it does what is for the advantage of another. In this sense it is the whole of virtue (*Nicomachean Ethics*

5.1.15-19).[2] (This is not far from Paul's functional definition of love: seeking the advantage of the other rather than your own [1 Cor. 10:24, 33; Phil. 2:4; 1 Thess. 5:15]. Interestingly enough, Aristotle and Paul use the same Greek word root to signify "advantage.")

Aristotle speaks of particular justice as of two kinds: distributive, and corrective or retributive (*NE* 5.2.1, 12, 13). Note three points:

1. For Aristotle, the authoritative ground of justice is the voice (law) of the political community. The legislature decides what is lawful—the rules of justice. Justice can exist only in the city, where mutual relations are regulated by law (*NE* 5.1.12-13; 6.4). *The gods do not establish justice*, or make contracts: they are supremely happy in their contemplation and neither sleep nor engage in activities toward human beings (*NE* 10.8.7).

2. Distributive justice is exercised in the distribution of honor, wealth, and other divisible assets from the common stock of the community (*NE* 5.2.12; 5.4.2). The principle of distribution is desert or merit, and the distribution that one deserves is proportionate to one's contribution to the community. (Aristotle recognizes that there are different opinions about what constitutes desert—wealth, free birth—but for him it is virtue [*NE* 1.7.14-15; 1.9.8-9; 5.3.7; 5.4.2].) Justice occurs as fairness when people who have made equal contributions to the community receive equal shares of the distribution. Injustice results when equal people receive unequal shares, or unequal people receive equal shares (*NE* 5.1.1, 8, 11; 5.3.3, 6, 14; 5.5.17; 5.6.4).

3. The purpose of retributive justice is to correct mistakes made in the distribution system.

The law treats the parties as equals and, looking at the damage, asks whether one has done injustice to another. The judge endeavors to equalize an unjust, that is, unequal, situation by imposing a penalty to take away the undue gain of the one who has received more good and less evil than is deserved (*NE* 5.5.2, 12; 5.4.2-8).

The Old Testament

These three aspects of justice take different shape in the Old Testament.

1. For Israel, the ground, authority, and model for justice is the exodus event, in which God liberated Israel from slavery and gave them freedom, land, and sustenance that they would not otherwise have had. God chose to bestow this favor upon Israel without regard for any merit or desert on Israel's part. God entered into a covenant relationship with Israel (Exod. 6:2-8; 19:4-5; 34:27; Deut. 6:20-25; 7:7-9), and thereby established God's own justice and righteousness (Ps. 99:4; Isa. 5:16; 61:8). Israel, then, is to manifest this same kind of justice in their communal life (Exod. 22:21; 23:9; Amos 5:7, 15, 24; Isa. 5:7). *Justice* occurs in the covenant community when everyone's rights are upheld, and *righteousness* defines those rights as deriving from a relationship. Israelites have a right to receive a distribution of the goods of society.[3] Israel's understanding of distributive justice has the closest connection to grace.

2. The liberating and redemptive activity of God also defines the principle of distribution in Israelite justice. Distribution is not based on moral desert (as in Aristotle) but on God's liberating action

for the Hebrew slaves in Egypt, and thus it demonstrates a special concern for the most vulnerable members of society—widows, orphans, the oppressed, the poor, resident aliens (Exod. 22:22; Deut. 10:18; Pss. 10:18; 94:3-6; Isa. 1:23; 3:15; Jer. 5:28). This preference for the poor does not mean that there are two different standards of justice, one for the rich and another for the poor: in fact there are laws that forbid favoring either (Exod. 23:6; Deut. 1:17; Lev. 19:15). It rather means that the justice system is formulated to fit the social conditions it is intended to serve. The poor are singled out for special concern because in actuality they have not received impartial treatment in their struggle with the rich. Social goods and power have been unequally and destructively distributed so that it is necessary for those who have too much to give up something for the sake of those who do not have enough.[4]

3. The relationship in the Old Testament between distributive and retributive justice is more complex. Some scholars have even questioned whether the Old Testament actually has a doctrine of divine retribution. Because of its centrality to my concern, we must examine this question at greater length.

The Question of Retribution in the Old Testament

Walter Brueggemann acknowledges that both distributive and retributive justice are attested in the Old Testament, but maintains that the distributive is clearly dominant and more characteristic. He connects retributive justice to merit, performance, the *lex talionis* ("an eye for an eye"), and the desire of the elite to maintain the present order for their benefit. He thus seems to see the two kinds of justice as quite different from each other and as logically unconnected. They are for him apparently two different ways of grasping the whole of justice, a kind of either/or.[5] I argue otherwise, that they are logically and necessarily connected to each other and that together they constitute the whole of justice.

In any human society there will always be injustices in the distribution of the community's goods; therefore, if the community is serious about distributive justice—and both ancient Greece and ancient Israel were—it will have to be just as serious about retributive justice, correcting inequality in distributing goods. For both Aristotle and the Old Testament, retributive justice exists to correct mistakes made in the distribution system. But the parallel here is only formal or logical, not material. For Aristotle, justice originates from the legislative voice of the political community, and the injured person is restored to a situation of equal distribution *for equal performance or contribution to society*. In the Old Testament, justice originates from God, and the injured person is restored to a position of equality *in a covenant community in which all have equal access to unmerited favor*, which in social terms means sufficient material resources to be a free and fully participating member of the community. In the area of social sins, when equal people receive unequal distributions, retributive justice means that the one who received too much must be penalized. Those who have summer houses and winter houses or virtually unlimited land, when others have nothing, must take a big loss (Isa. 5:8-10; Amos 3:15). Religious sin entails that only God is to be exalted, but human beings, in their inequality, seek to elevate themselves to equality with God, and as a result are brought low (Isa. 2: 12, 17).

Distributive justice as unmerited favor, and equal access to this apart from right performance, are central to the Old Testament. The purpose of retributive justice is to restore equality in Israel when it has been violated. But there is also a contrary strand in which, although distributive justice is based on *unmerited favor*, retributive justice becomes a matter of reward for obedient performance and punishment for the lack thereof. Hosea can speak in poignant terms of God's tender love for Israel but also of God's punishment of Israel's rebellion, expressed in terms of the *lex talionis* (4:6; 8:7; 12:14). Deuteronomy affirms that God has chosen Israel out of God's love and not for any desert on Israel's part, yet Israel is required to maintain herself in the land and purge her guilt by right actions (4:1; 6:18; 7:12; 8:1; 11:26-28; 16:20; 21:9; 27:11-26; 28:15-68). This motif of theological legalism—good works as the condition for salvation—can be seen in many other places (Job 34:11; Pss. 18:20-24; 62:12; Prov. 24:12; Jer.17:10; Hos. 12:2; Tob. 4:9-10; Sir. 16:12-14), and is evident in the New Testament as well: Paul, the very fountainhead of justification by grace through faith, nevertheless speaks of judgment by good works (Rom. 14:10-12; 2 Cor. 5:10). And this tendency takes on a more programmatic clarity in Matthew, where, although grace is a reality that enables the appropriate human response, performance nevertheless appears at key points (5:20; 6:14-15; 7:24-25; 16:27; 18:35) as the condition for salvation.

Rather than eliminating either side of this biblical tension between distributive justice, based on unconditional acceptance by God, and retributive justice, based on human performance, let us suppose that it is grounded in the experience of those who have lived out of this biblical tradition. The tension is not between our experience of the love of God and of the justice of God but rather between two aspects of God's love. On the one hand, we experience God's love as unconditional acceptance without regard for our performance or desert but, on the other hand, we experience God's love as the *demand* that we actualize the best possibilities for which we have been created and as the *cost* of disobeying that demand. Both of these two differing kinds of love express God's concern for our well-being. We are not able to rationalize the gap between these two different experiences of love, but both are real, so we maintain the tension and learn to live with it.

While Walter Brueggemann questioned whether retribution appears with legitimacy in the Old Testament, Klaus Koch questions whether it appears there at all. In his view, retribution has four defining features: (1) There is a judicial process (2) governed by a higher authority (3) who imposes a consequence—punishment or reward—from outside, rather than as an intrinsic outflow from a person's actions. (4) The basis for this judicial decision is a pre-established norm.[6]

Koch denies that any of these factors appears in the Old Testament except for the presiding higher authority—God.[7] I disagree. As for a "judicial process," I agree with Walter Brueggemann's contention that the whole of Old Testament theology can be embraced by the rhetorical form of testimony, specifically Israel's testimony about God. But the social context for testimony is the court of law, where witnesses are assembled to give account of a reality in question. All utterance in the Old Testament about God, even that placed in the mouth of God, has a human speaker as its writer or source, and the lawcourt is the premier context in which Israel's language evokes Israel's God.[8] We see this, for example, in Isaiah's song of the vineyard (5:1-7), which has its proper setting, as David Carr has suggested, in the city gate where legal cases are contested.[9] Again, we see the court setting in Mic. 6:1-2, where it seems God is being indicted by Israel, and presses a counter-charge in return.

As to Koch's denial that the Old Testament speaks of retribution as punishment imposed from the outside, I note that in the Book of the Covenant, both laws and the punishments for breaking them are set forth by Yahweh (Exod. 20:22). When these punishments take the form of the death penalty, or of financial restitution as much as five times greater than the damage (Exod. 22:1), handed down by judicial decree (Exod. 21:22) or by God (Exod. 22:24), then we clearly have something imposed, not flowing "naturally" from a person's own actions. Similarly, the language of acquittal or its opposite evokes both a court procedure and the externality of the punishment: God will not acquit the guilty (Exod. 23:7), nor are human judges to do so (Prov. 17:15; Isa. 5:23). Again, whenever the prophets describe judgment occurring by means of a foreign invader rather than as the result of an internal disintegrative process, we may speak of punishment from outside (see Chapter 1).

As to Koch's denial of a pre-established norm as the basis for judgment, I find this very much present in the Old Testament. For example, in Hos. 6:7; 8:1, Israel is condemned for transgressing a very broad and inclusive norm—the covenant and the law. More specifically Israel has violated the commandments against worshiping other gods and making idols (Hos. 2:8; 4:12-13, 17). The Decalogue itself announces punishment for idolatry (Exod. 20:4-6; Deut. 5:8-10). Jeremiah vividly promises judgment against Israel for violating both the Decalogue and principles of social justice—concern for the most vulnerable (Jer. 7:1-15). Isaiah pronounces judgment against those who have expropriated the land of others (Isa. 5:8-10), a very specific concern of social justice that is enshrined in the law codes (Lev. 25:23; Deut. 19:14).

Koch's primary concern is the biblical affirmation of an inevitable, organic connection between a person's actions and their consequences (Pss. 34:21; 37:1-2, 14-15; 59:12-13; 107:17-18; Prov. 11:1, 3-6, 17-21, 27, 30-31; 26:28; 28:1, 10, 17; 29:6; Hos. 5:4; 8:4-7). God's role in this unbreakable connection is not merely an internal or subjective response to human behavior; rather in some sense God intervenes, completes the inherent connection between action and consequence, turns the effects of one's actions back on the actor, and abandons the person to the consequences. Koch insists, however, that God does not negate the built-in action-consequence sequence and does not introduce punishment. (Koch does acknowledge that in the Psalms God's role is somewhat more interventionist than elsewhere, for without God the process would not get started.)[10]

For Koch, in the end, the process seems more essential than God's involvement in it. The configuration of action and consequence is like a law of nature, and God is like a catalyst that speeds up a chemical process already begun.[11] God is something of an addendum—extrinsic, not integral. But John Barton rightly denies that the sequence of deed and consequence is presented in the Old Testament as operating automatically, and that God's role is limited to somehow keeping the system going without intervening. In Isa. 5:8-9, for example, God does act to punish the violation of a moral norm in such a way that the punishment (loss of land) fits the sin (the unjustified expropriation of land). God's moral character is thus revealed as consistent and rational in dealing with us.[12]

Furthermore, Old Testament narrative offers us a clearer picture of the interaction between human action and God's purposes in history than comes to light in Koch's analysis. In the Joseph story we have a series of deceptions and cruelties directed against Joseph by his brothers, to which he ultimately responds by renouncing vengeance in favor of forgiveness. The irreducible coincidence of both human freedom and intentions, and the providence of God, is evident in Joseph's words to his brothers at the end: God sent me to preserve life, to keep you alive, so it was not you but God who sent me here (Gen. 45:5-8). You intended to do me harm, but God intended it for good (Gen. 50:20).

Similarly, in the Davidic Succession Narrative (2 Sam. 9–20; 1 Kgs. 1–2) there are, as John Barton put it, two parallel plots. In one, God determines that Solomon shall sit on David's throne; in the other, we have free, unforced human action, the conniving among David's sons and others about the succession—a chain of human causation. The first is the theological interpretation of the second. The two mysteriously have the same result. Just deserts merge with inscrutable divine providence and with unintended bad consequences of good acts. There is, however, no divine intervention; rather the divine hand is hidden behind the normal processes of human history.[13]

These narratives allow us to state the paradoxical relationship between human action and divine judgment in history more sharply and clearly than Koch has done. Human history unfolds realistically, with the participants acting with as much freedom as is possible for finite creatures. They reflect, choose, act, and deal with consequences both intended and unintended. Some of their projects diminish their freedom and constrict their possibilities, generating blindness and hardness of heart. Divine action coincides with this human history, is interwoven with it. In significant strands of the Old Testament, divine action is not invasive but is rather hidden in the dynamics of human history—personal, national, and international. The fusion of the two, divine and human action, does not diminish the reality of either. Both are fully operative. That does not mean that they are equal, for the divine and human are never equal in the Bible, but both are fully present as what they are.

I conclude that the Old Testament expresses a strong concept of retributive justice. Koch pays no attention to the equalizing function of retributive justice; nor does he note the *logical* connection between distributive and retributive justice, which requires the latter if the former is taken seriously.

Some Particulars of Biblical Justice

I turn now from these more general questions of justice to consider a few specific rules and implications of distributive justice in the Old Testament.

1. The maintenance of justice is the responsibility of both *rulers* (2 Sam. 8:15; 1 Kgs. 10:9; Isa. 32:1; Jer. 22:1-4; Mic. 3:9-12) and *people* (Exod. 22:21; 23:1-2; 6; Deut. 10:12-13, 17-19; Isa. 5:7). It requires the king's activity in legislation and litigation and the good will of the people.[14]

2. There must be *laws* that make social justice possible and prevent injustice (Ps. 94:3-6, 20-21; Isa. 10:1-2).

3. The entrance gates of the towns were the centers of Israel's political, judicial, and commercial life. Both laws and prophetic protests sought to protect the poor from being victimized in court by false charges or the bribing of judges (Exod. 23:1-2, 6, 8; Deut. 16:19; 19:15-21; Isa. 1:23, 5:23, Amos 5:12; Mic. 3:9-11; 6:11-12), and from being cheated in the marketplace by the use of unjust measures and weights (Deut. 25:13-5; Lev. 19:35-36; Amos 8:4-5; Mic. 6:10-11). This concern with economic and judicial *insitutions* of the city shows that Israelite distributive justice was truly *social* justice.

4. The prophets strongly criticized the pursuit of excess luxury and the accumulation of wealth and status (Isa. 32: 9-14; Jer. 17:11; Amos 3:15; 4:1; 6:1, 4-7; Mic. 3: 9-11).

5. Workers were to be paid what they were due (Deut. 24:14-5; Jer. 22:13-4).

6. Israelite justice upheld the right of a family to its land, which belonged ultimately to God who allotted it in trust to families (Lev. 25:23; Deut. 19:14). A family's land was not to be sold out of the family in perpetuity, nor was anyone to remove long-standing boundary markers (Lev. 25:23; Deut. 19:14). The prophets inveighed against the rich, who crushed the poor by seizing the fields of those who could not pay their mortgages (Isa. 3:14-5; Jer. 17:11; Mic. 2:1-2). As Waldemar Janzen has observed, the Old Testament concern with land goes beyond its most literal sense: land provided a specific place to live; it was the physical and emotional foundation for life, and the means of production and security. This concern for the land should not be limited to an agricultural setting.[15] Yet Old Testament protections for the family in possession of land are not absolute. Gleaning laws (Deut. 24:19-22; Lev. 23:22) and laws allowing a person to satisfy momentary hunger in someone else's vineyard or grain field (Deut. 23:24-25) both relativize the right to private property. So do sabbath year laws, which require that the land should not be cultivated so that the poor may eat from it, and the Jubilee Year provisions for canceling debts, freeing slaves, and restoring land to original owners (Lev. 25).

7. These and other similar demands make clear that no one in Israel is to be in need (Exod. 16: 17-18; Deut. 15:4-11). All Israelites, including especially

the weak and vulnerable, are to be enabled to have a full life, and to participate in the community.[16] The combined concerns with protecting the deprived and criticizing excessive luxury and wealth show that, in the Old Testament, social justice requires reducing the gulf between rich and poor and moving toward equality.

It should be noted that the prophets call for justice *between* nations as well as domestic justice within Israel, and apply the same principles there. Just as a family is forbidden to seize the land of another, so a nation is forbidden to expropriate the land of another or to violate its integrity. This kind of international behavior brings judgment (Amos 1:6, 13).

What, Then, of the United States?

Ancient Israel believed that both the nature of justice and the demand for it rested on the revelation of God. The United States, on the other hand, may fairly be described (at least constitutionally) as a pluralistic and secular state whose justice system is politically grounded apart from a basis in revelation. Are there any biblical grounds for holding secular states accountable to the biblical understanding of justice?

I argue yes, on the basis of two biblical themes. First, Amos seems to assume that *all* nations know God's demand for justice in international relations. John Barton argues that in holding the nations responsible, Amos is appealing to popular belief, a kind of conventional law about international conduct, and that Amos's audience probably heard nothing deeply theological here.[17] However, if Amos is appropriating conventional beliefs, he nevertheless makes God the ultimate source of them. All the oracles in Amos 1–2 begin with "thus says the Lord," and the Lord speaks in the first person throughout. Amos seems to imply that the universal revelation of God's justice occurs in the varying transactions of human historical experience.

Note that in the oracles in Amos 1–2, Judah is judged for rejecting the law of the Lord (2:4–5) and Israel for religious (2:8, 10, 12) as well as social sins. However, the other nations are judged only for sins of the social and political order. The prophet makes a distinction in principle here. The deeds for which the other nations are condemned are (1) brutality in war (1:3, 13; 2:1); (2) the removal of people from their own land (1:6); (3) a country's enlarging its own territory at the expense of another (1:13); and (4) acts regarded as violations of brotherhood (1:9, 11), probably indicating the violation of treaties.[18] That these actions are unjust and wicked is, then, the content of the "natural revelation" that is accessible to the nations, that which the nations can know from their own historical experience and which is not dependent on a special salvation history or covenant such as Israel had. This bears, I contend, on what repentance would mean for the United States in the international arena.

Second, for the Old Testament, the divine sense of justice has been enshrined in the very creation of the world and thus is available to all (Pss. 33:4–7; 89:2, 10–14; Isa. 45:18–19, 23–24). This makes creation a cosmos, a habitable place, not a chaos.[19]

These two motifs justify our claiming that from the biblical standpoint the United States can be held accountable to the Old Testament understanding of justice.

3.

The People under Judgment: A Biblical Motif

In the previous chapter I discussed, primarily at the conceptual or philosophical level, the nature of retributive justice—judgment—and argued that it does in fact appear prominently in the Old Testament, indeed, that it is integral to Israel's understanding of the whole of justice. Here I will look more concretely at how and why judgment occurs, and consider some of the implications of grasping the events of 9/11 under the theme of judgment.

The Prophetic Theological Context of Judgment

Stated summarily, judgment comes because of both Israel's arrogance toward God (Isa. 1:2; 2:8, 11-12; 9:8-12) and its injustice within the covenant community (Isa. 1:17, 21, 24-25; 5:7; Amos 2:6; 5:15, 24). I generalize the following characteristic emphases of the prophets from John Barton's insightful analysis of the organizing principles of Isaiah's ethics, based on Isa. 2:6–22; 3:1–12; 5:8–10; 5:20; and 29:15–16.[1]

1. The cosmos is a hierarchically ordered whole, with God alone at the top and human beings and nature at lower positions. This is implicit in the proclamation that only God is to be exalted (Isa. 2:14, 17) and in the critique of turning order into disorder (5:20; 29:15–16).

2. All are called to acknowledge the sovereignty of God. This comprehensive imperative means that human beings are to accept their appointed place in the cosmic order. When they do not, they lose their bearings on reality and descend into a vicious circular dialectic of arrogance and ignorance (1:3; 5:13, 20–21). It is hardly possible to say which comes first. Arrogance—placing oneself too high, attaching excessive worth to oneself—causes people to have a distorted view of reality—ignorance, blindness, misunderstanding (1:3; 5:13, 20–21); and ignorance or blindness to the order of reality causes people to attribute undue value to themselves—arrogance.

Isa. 5:20 and 29:15–16 illuminate the fusion of arrogance and blindness. The people under judgment here are those who reverse or turn upside down the order of the world—making evil good; darkness light; bitter sweet. This causes the devastation of the society's life-support system (3:1; 5:8–19) and introduces political chaos (3:2–8). The ultimate overturning is the attempt of the human creature to replace the divine creator. Those who foolishly think that their dark plans and deeds can escape the notice of God presume to take the role of the potter and reduce God to the clay.

3.   Pride and ignorance produce harmful and ruinous acts of injustice (1:4, 13, 16-17; 3:14-15; 5:8-10; 14:4-6, 12-17, 20; 19:11, 14-15).

Prophetic Judgment and the Tower of Babel

The Tower of Babel (Gen. 11:1-9) is an interesting case for our examination for several reasons. Although it is a striking example of prophetic judgment *outside* of the prophetic writings, the oracle of judgment in Isa. 9:8-17 seems to allude powerfully to it. Isaiah's oracle speaks of God's judgment against an arrogant Israel that seeks to ground its security in a city that it will build or rebuild. Beyond this broad similarity, the connection between the Genesis story of the Tower of Babel and the oracle of judgment in Isaiah is reinforced by specific building vocabulary in Isaiah that echoes the Genesis story, and, most interestingly, by the introduction, in the LXX (Greek) version of the Isaiah passage, of a tower—which the Hebrew (and English) versions do not have—into the city. The LXX version of 9:8-10 may be translated as follows: "The Lord sent death upon Jacob and it came upon Israel, and all the people of Ephraim and those couched in Samaria knowingly will say, with arrogance and a haughty heart: 'bricks have fallen, but come let us hew stones, let us cut sycamores and cedars, *and let us build ourselves a tower.*'" The italicized phrase echoes Gen. 11:4. The Tower of Babel is allusively present in Isaiah's oracle.

Of course, the Genesis story is especially intriguing because the graphic visual similarity between the biblical tower and the Twin Towers in New York invites reflection: are there connections beyond the merely symbolic between the two structures?

In Genesis 11, the tower and its city represent the human desire to become equal to God—building a tower reaching to heaven—and secure in our cultural achievements. This is the social extension of the sin of Adam: the attempt to rival God. According to Genesis, the Lord did not look with favor upon this enterprise and put an end to it.

And what of the towers in New York? The long, complex process leading to the building of the Twin Towers probably owed more to David Rockefeller and his initiative vision than to any other one person. Historians of the towers observe that their builders were possessed by a determination that often crossed over into hybris. No problem would keep them from building the world's tallest skyscraper: not the bitter, displaced shopkeepers; not natural forces, economics, politics, civic hostility, legal challenges, or engineering doubts. Only after 9/11 was it remembered that, early on, opponents had warned that an airplane strike or a large fire could cause the huge structures to collapse. For Rockefeller and his team, the complex was to serve as a place where the United States and foreign interests could meet for mutual consultation and business transactions. Such a center would accelerate the development of international business and act as a symbol of this country's growing world leadership. The towers thus came to signify unbridled chutzpah.[2]

Despite initial opposition, the Twin Towers gradually worked their way into the affections of ordinary New Yorkers, and eventually of Americans, as they were the biggest, brashest icons New York ever produced.[3] The nation itself would mourn, not just the lives lost, but the towers themselves. The extent to which devotion to this icon had penetrated the psyche of city, nation, and church can be seen in one of the sermons preached in New York City on the Sunday after 9/11, in which the minister gave voice to his awe and wonder that the human mind could create such extraordinary structures. The towers were the symbol of American free enterprise. Where do we look for meaning when we have lost such an important symbol, when we have lost—as *Time* put it, without irony—"America's Cathedrals?"[4]

Note, in summary, three themes in the biblical story: (1) the Tower of Babel was built by pride; (2) the tower took a hit; (3) Genesis interprets the hit as the judging action of God. The 9/11 events, in a different social context, clearly parallel the first two motifs: (1) the Twin Towers were built by pride; (2) the towers took a hit. The comparison invites the question, what about the third motif? Should 9/11 also be interpreted as the judging action of God?

Judgment and the Problem of Contingency

When the prophets proclaim judgment, they often introduce a note of contingency into the threat. If Israel repents and turns from faithlessness to faithfulness and from injustice to justice, then God will turn away the punishment (Isa. 1:19-20; Jer. 3:12-22; 4:1-4, 14; 7:5-7; Amos 5:4, 6,15). When the judgment is portrayed as destructive invasion by a foreign power (Isa. 1:5-9; 10:3, 5-11; Jer. 4:6-8; Amos 4:2-3; 4:10; 7:11-17), we may, in retrospect, regard this note of contingency as implausible. Would a change of heart on the part of Israel have had any impact on the imperialistic intentions of Assyria (Isa. 10:5-11)? I think not. The ravaging strike would have occurred anyway. Clearly, for Isaiah the Assyrian king is the agent of God's judgment but, just as clearly, the king had no awareness of this, for his only intention was to conquer (Isa. 10:5-11). With considerable theological sophistication Isaiah suggests the paradoxical position that God achieves God's purposes in history without destroying the freedom and semi-autonomy of God's instruments.

If judgment-as-invasion is going to come regardless of what Israel might do, then what meaning and effect could repentance have? Is it possible to interpret judgment in such a way that repentance would take on significance, existential substance, a genuine chance to change the situation under judgment?

Isaiah has in fact developed a more realistic and hopeful position, in considerable concrete detail. In 3:1-17, judgment takes the form of the disappearance of social life-support systems, the breakdown of domestic order, and the failure of leadership. Military, judicial, and religious officials have vanished; adults refuse to lead so that babies are the rulers; and everyone oppresses everyone. But this is not an offense calling for punishment: this *is* the punishment. The social disparity between the rich and poor, caused by the injustice of the rich, explodes intrinsically into general chaos and anarchy. This is still God's judging action (3:1), but God carries out God's purpose, not by using an invader from outside, but by working secretly through Israel's own disintegrative behavior. The people have brought it on themselves (3:9). When judgment is so understood—then or now—a repentant turn to justice could indeed change things and reverse the ruinous disorder.

Hosea, also, may hint at the idea of judgment as the climax of a disintegrative process in 5:8-11, where God does not use a foreign conqueror to bring judgment, but acts as the hidden power in Israel's self-induced process of decay. "Therefore I am like maggots to Ephraim, and like rottenness to the house of Judah" (5:12, NRSV).

In Chapter 1 I discussed the relationship between judgment as divine disruption of ordinary history and as the explosive culmination of an ongoing history in which God is present, though hidden. The intervention "from above" becomes a metaphor that focalizes the hidden presence of God as a visible presence. But metaphorical truth, arresting and revealing as it may be, is not literal truth. When we look back on biblical claims of divine judgment or contemplate the possibility that events of our time could be acts of judgment, we should understand them all in this de-literalized, metaphorical way. There is no direct intervention "from above."

Yet when we move from the hermeneutical question—our attempt to understand the nature of divine involvement—to lived political reality, isn't there a difference between disaster caused by an agent from outside the nation and disaster caused by a process of decay inside the nation's social, economic, and political history? How might we speak of the relationship between these two judgments, from outside and from within?

There is more than one possibility. Judgment as invasion and as internal disintegration might occur independently of each other. Or they could be connected in an organic, that is, a political and existential way. If a nation were divided and conflicted because of an unacceptable gulf between the rich and the poor, that might make the nation an easier prey for an ambitious enemy than it would otherwise be.

Jared Diamond has reflected on this issue, using the fall of Rome as his example. He points out that what may appear to be the collapse of a nation from invasion may owe more to internal disintegration thatn meets the eye.[5] Since the connection between external and internal forces can be inherent in some situations, the prophets may have been less naive than they appear to have been when they call on Israel to repent of domestic injustice in order to avoid conquest by an invader.

Having looked at justice and judgment in light of these biblical and philosophical considerations, I turn now to ask about the meaning of 9/11 from two quite different perspectives.

4.

9/11 as an Evil Committed
by al-Qaeda

The Problem of Evil

I see 9/11 paradoxically as both an undeserved evil perpetrated against us and as a judgment imposed on us because of our own injustice. The events of that day were profoundly evil, and the horror should not be minimized. As Jim Wallis put it, we should not think of the 9/11 terrorists as freedom fighters who went too far, but rather as perverted religious fundamentalists who were pursuing regional and global power and a new religious and political empire of their own. They would destroy democracy, deny human rights, repress women, and persecute people of other faiths and even fellow-believers who disagree with them.[1]

But what does it mean to describe the events of 9/11 as "evil"? In this chapter I reflect on the nature of evil in relation to judgment, and more specifically ask whether in the biblical tradition evil *as evil* is ever thought of as serving God's purposes. I then suggest a way Christians might respond not just to 9/11 but to other manifestations of evil.

The dimensions of suffering imposed in New York and Washington and over Pennsylvania were abominable, and the people who suffered were no more guilty than the rest of us. So we may be tempted to identify with Dostoevsky's Ivan Karamazov, who after his agonized litany about innocent suffering said that he would hasten to give God back his entrance ticket. Ivan rejects not God but the way that God has arranged the world so as to allow the suffering of innocent children. And Ivan vehemently repudiates the view that such suffering could be justified or made reasonable or acceptable by understanding it as contributing to the achievement of a grand cosmic harmony at some remote future time. There is no truth that will be able to show what the suffering has all been for.[2]

At the outset I wish to distinguish the theological question of evil from historical questions about responsibility for 9/11. It has generally been assumed that the perpetrators of the evil acts on 9/11 were al-Qaeda and its agents, but that may not be all of the truth. David Griffin's *The New Pearl Harbor* has presented an impressive array of evidence that challenges the official story of the 9/11 event. That evidence suggests some degree of complicity on the part of the Bush government in allowing 9/11 to happen, motivated by the need for a "new Pearl Harbor" to galvanize the American people into a willingness to pursue a cluster of military ventures, including the Iraqi war. This motive is documented in the Project for the New American Century's *Rebuilding America's Defenses* and in the report of the "Rumsfeld Commission" published in January, 2001.[3] If Griffin's evidence and arguments prove to be convincing, we may have to revise our judgment about who all the agents of 9/11 were. That would, of course, enlarge and complicate our conception of the full identity of the agency of destruction, but it would not materially change the discussion of the theological problem of evil.

Evil has always been a problem for Christian theology. If God is good (wills the well-being of humankind) and also powerful (has the capability to maintain that well-being of humankind), where does evil come from? Theodicy in the Western tradition has characteristically sought to justify God in explaining how evil could happen. If God is good and yet evil happens, God must lack power. If God is powerful and yet evil happens, God must lack love. But how can God be both loving and powerful, as the Christian tradition affirms, yet evil happens?

With all the talk about evil since 9/11, especially from the Bush administration and its supporters, there has been little effort to clarify exactly what we mean by the word. The dominant public rhetoric, as Mark Lewis Taylor has analyzed it,[4] displays three major themes: (1) Terrorism is the great evil, understood as sudden attacks against the U.S., at home or abroad, that harm civilians or military personnel; (2) The nation is called to be "against" this evil; (3) The nation's very core is interpreted as opposing this evil which defines our time. Each of these themes is a simplistic narrowing of vision. The first deflects our attention from other evils (racism, health care, environment). The second directs us away from being *for* something. And the third reduces the complexity of "our time" to the war against terrorism.

We need to think more critically about what we mean when we say that we have been dealt an evil blow and about how we should respond to this as Christians, and as Americans. The following discussion will take up the topic of a theological-faith response to the occurrence of evil, while Chapter 9 will address the nature of an appropriate ethical response to 9/11 in its various dimensions.

What Is Evil?

In his recent book *Responding to Evil*, Joseph Kelly[5] argues that although we cannot ultimately define evil precisely, we recognize it when we see it. In order to discuss it at all, we need a working definition. He appeals to Jeffrey Burton Russell: evil is "the deliberate imposition of suffering by a human being upon another sentient being." (The harm need not be limited to the physical.) We might also tease a working definition of evil out of Gordon Graham's recent *Evil and Christian Ethics*, where Graham argues that, because slavery is something that the modern world universally condemns, it provides us a basis for moral thinking about evil. The evil in slavery is that it turns persons into objects, the property of others; persons are not treated as ends in themselves, but as means to the ends of their owners. This dehumanizes both the master and the slave. Although there are people today who are quite prepared to perpetuate social arrangements that are hardly distinguishable from slavery, no one expressly advocates slavery.[6] We recognize slavery as evil, then, because it nullifies the personhood of the other, and in so doing subverts the self-interest and the well-being of the agent of evil, the victim, and the society as a whole.[7]

In her stimulating *Evil in Modern Thought*, Susan Neiman maintains that no definition of evil can be given: there is no essence of evil that stays constant over the historical course of its changing manifestations. It cannot be defined in such a way that we will always be able to recognize it, nor is there any criterion for distinguishing evil from the "awful" or the "very bad."[8] This does not mean, however, that we must flounder in irremediable ignorance and uncertainty regarding evil, nor does she deny that we may be certain about particular, paridigmatic instances of evil.[9]

Neiman identifies certain specific actions or events as evil: torture, Auschwitz, 9/11. While the al-Qaeda attacks seem to us acts of unmitigated, "old-fashioned" evil—the sheer and deliberate attempt to cause as much death, havoc, and fear as possible—they were quite modern in their technological execution.[10] Since Neiman has denied that evil has a definable essence that enables us to recognize its occurrence with clarity, on what grounds can she make these identifications?

For Neiman, designating something as evil has more to do with *its effect on us* than with its cause. We define evil by what it does to us. To call an action evil is to suggest that it cannot be fitted into an established structure of meaning; therefore it is unlike crime, which can be comprehended in our judicial order. *Evil* threatens our very trust in the world, our sense of a coherent order that we need in order to orient ourselves. The events of 9/11 were evil in this sense: They were a historical turning point that caused the ground that we depend on—our ability to navigate the world—to vanish, or at least become infinitely more precarious.[11]

Neiman's position is in part convincing, but contains some tensions. Her consequentialist understanding of evil is useful as a description of some occurrences of it, but is it comprehensive and precise enough to serve as a definition? Would it, for example, rule out as evil a brutal, intentional slaughter of only one hundred people that, however horrible, did not shatter our sense of order and cause a thoroughgoing disorientation?

Occasionally, Neiman slips deconstructively into making or implying a point that has been ruled out logically by her primary position; that is, she occasionally seems to assume a more nearly essentialist definition of evil. It is an error, she states, to understand Auschwitz as analogous to an earthquake, or terrorism as a virus.[12] She believes it unjustified to try to grasp moral evil by the use of seismological or biological metaphors. But this implies a definition not on the basis of effect, but on the basis of cause or nature.

Do these tensions in Neiman's position not prompt us to consider whether there might not be an essentialist definition of evil—an identifiable meaning that is not fixed but rather posits a *reservoir of possibility* that can generate different manifestations in changing times and situations? The reservoir has indistinct borders, but it does impose some limits on the magnitude of change that can take place in the nature of evil if the manifestations are to be at all recognizable as variants of a common point of origin and as legitimate referents of the same word—*evil.*

The content of this flexible and adaptable reservoir of semantic possibility would understand evil as harm and suffering visited upon humans and other sentient beings. With regard to humans, it would include physical, existential, and psychological harm. Slavery in its gross and subtle forms, any deprivation of the freedom required to be human, would be close to the essence of evil. But, given historical and cultural change, designating any particular phenomenon as evil requires an interpretive judgment, and such judgments resist objective certainty. I hold that evil does have an open-ended meaning but that our identifications of particular evils are not absolutely sure.

I have not explicitly stated a position on the question of natural evil. Are earthquakes or tsunamis evil? If evil is defined solely on the basis of the agent's consciousness—the intention to cause harm and suffering—then there is no natural evil, since nature, presumably, has no subjective intentions. But is this a reductionist definition? There is obviously no evil without a victim, and if the suffering of the victim is not excluded but is given its proportional place in the definition, then the difference between personal and natural evil is diminished. They have the suffering victim in common. Thus, on the basis of my interpretive judgment that a definition of evil should comprehend both agent and victim, I affirm the reality of natural evil.

Evil and the Mystery of God in the Bible

In Luke 13:1-5, Jesus speaks of personal evil (Pilate's slaughter of the Galileans) and natural evil (the fall of the Tower of Siloam on eighteen Jerusalemites) in parallel terms, as if there were no categorical difference between them. He tells some questioners that the people killed when the Tower of Siloam fell on them were not worse sinners than the rest of Jerusalem. The story gives no explanation for their suffering: indeed, Jesus expressly denies that they suffered because of their sin, nor does he blame it on satanic forces. I suppose he implies that the problem should be left to God's mysterious dealing, since he refuses to assign a clear cause for their deaths. But he does strongly urge the questioners to repent lest the same fate befall them. If we juxtapose the events of 9/11not only with the Tower of Babel but also with the Tower of Siloam, perhaps we will find ourselves confronted with the question: have we heard the warning?

Walter Brueggemann has shown very pointedly that in the Old Testament, theodicy is not explanation or justification but protest.[13] Israel's core testimony is that God graciously delivered Israel from slavery and entered into a covenant relationship in which both God and Israel would be faithful. Part and parcel of this covenant relationship is the "theodicy settlement" whose provisions affirm that obedience will bring life and peace, while disobedience will bring suffering and ruin, that is, punishment. The problem with this theo-ethical assertion was that often it did not fit life as actually lived. Therefore there arose in Israel a countertestimony in which Israel accuses Yahweh of not being faithful to Yahweh's own covenant commitments. The wicked prosper, and the righteous suffer. Sometimes the protest is against Yahweh's passive neglect in not preventing "the enemy" from causing the faithful to suffer (Pss. 3:1, 7; 5:8-9); at other times Israel charges Yahweh with being the direct and abusive cause of pain and suffering (Pss. 88:16-18; 39:5, 10; 44:9-15). In such passages there is no indication that the speaker feels guilty or that the punishment was deserved. Rather the faithfulness of Israel is asserted (Ps. 44:16-17). At the same time, however, Israel does not relinquish its testimony that God is just and demonstrates what justice is, and Israel frequently seeks to rouse Yahweh to manifest this justice (Pss. 3:1, 7; 44:23-26).

Brueggemann makes the important point that Israel in its honesty refused to allow that the disorder, injustice, and suffering in its life were always due to its own covenantal failure. Israel would not accept full fault when it believed that some of the fault belonged to "the enemy" or directly to Yahweh. Brueggemann further suggests that Christianity has generally lacked the nerve to incorporate this theme into its constructive theology.

As Brueggemann observes, Job faces these issues with a unique intensity. There is no rationally satisfying philosophical answer to the question Job poses in 21:7: Why do the wicked prosper? Nor do we get any comfort in the face of Job's accusation, from a slightly different perspective, that God treats both the blameless and the wicked to equal damage (9:22). The overwhelming God that Job does finally encounter in the whirlwind, however, stands above these easy calculations about who deserves what in the way of reward and punishment. Nothing is certain or settled when one stands before this God. Yet in the end, God answers Job, takes him seriously, and is available to him. Communion with God—the *existential* answer to Job's anguish—is a real possibility, despite the fact there is no philosophical clarity about the source or purpose of evil (38:1; 42:1-6).

For Brueggemann, maintaining the tensions between the *core* testimony—Yahweh is just and gracious and rewards in a morally coherent way— and the *countertestimony*—Yahweh is sometimes unreliable, abusive and unfaithful to the covenant—is an essential dimension of Old Testament theology and the faith of Israel. A believer who lived this faith would necessarily move back and forth between the two testimonies. Can we say more about the nature of such a faith?

Job believes that God has treated him unjustly, for he is a just and blameless man whom God has turned into a laughingstock, while God blesses the wicked (12:4-6). Job declares: God has worn me out, shriveled me up, torn and hated me (16:7-9); God has hunted me down with fresh troops (10:15-16); and God is to be held accountable for this, because God's hand is in everything (12:7-25). Although Job does not believe God would listen to him—even though he is innocent (9:15-16)—if he summoned God, he nevertheless calls for a hearing (13:3). After detailing the high moral standard by which he has always lived (13:1-34), Job calls again for God to grant him a hearing, believing that he would clearly carry the day against God.

He would confidently approach God like a prince (31:35-37)—for he *is* innocent (9:20-21; 27:5-6).

Later the voice of God sounds out of the whirlwind and sternly asks Job whether he, Job, has the creative, cosmic power to have brought the world into existence and to have cared for it (chaps. 38–39). Job is abashed and learns that he has still more questions to answer from God.

As Klaus Koch has pointed out, God's appearance has demonstrated that Job has neither the power nor knowledge to have created the world or to execute justice. Therefore, he is *not* God, and is in no position to try God or put God in the wrong (40:1-14), even though Job's complaints about God's injustice are valid. God is still committed to the action-consequence structure of justice (40:10-14), but God, as God, sometimes acts in an exceptional way, contrary to covenant expectations. Human beings do not have the power or knowledge to understand or question these exceptions.[14] If Job actually had the power and wisdom to do what God can and does do, then God would acknowledge that Job had won the judicial victory by his own capability—by his own right hand (40:14). But Job has been shown not to have that strong a right hand.

One implication of the Book of Job is that unexplained evil can be assigned, at least in part, to the mystery of God. Opposing this opinion in an interview in *The Christian Century*, David B. Hart has raised the question, "Where Was God in the Tsunami?"[15] Hart holds, first, that Scripture simply affirms that evil cannot defeat God's purpose or thwart the coming of the kingdom of God. It does not rationalize evil, and nowhere does it make evil a necessary part of God's achieving the realization of God's kingdom. Second, however, Hart apparently regards assigning evil to the mystery of God as simply another version of the effort to rationalize evil by making it a part of God's ultimate "greater plan."

I address these two contentions in reverse order. In Job 38–40 the mystery of God is portrayed from the standpoint of Job's deficiency. He lacks the knowledge to understand either the magnificence or the intricate complexity of God's cosmic and historical work, and he lacks the power to replicate it. On the other hand, the Bible can also present God's mystery from the standpoint of God's own inscrutable and unfathomable mind (Rom. 11:33–34; Isa. 40:13-14 [LXX]; 55:8-9). The mind of God is unbreachable: there is an impenetrable beyond. This stance provides a horizon against which we can include several affirmations of faith that are not necessarily logically consistent: (1) God has shown what justice is, has commanded it of us, and is still committed to it; (2) but God sometimes troublingly deviates from the rules of justice; (3) we have permission to protest this; (4) but we lack the wisdom and power to call God to trial. (5) We nevertheless have reason to hope for the final victory of love and justice.

Biblical affirmations about the mystery of God enable us to affirm all of these things because this mystery entails a dimension that we cannot access, in which things that seem incompatible to us in our finitude might fit together. But (contra Hart) this position does not commit us to hold that the eschatological resolution will show that evil does in fact fit harmoniously into and contribute to God's grand design. We can remain agnostic on that point. We believe in God's victorious eschatological redemption, but we do not know whether that will make sense of evil.

The Subjective Experience of Evil: Job and Paul

I return to Hart's first point: is it really so clear that the biblical tradition never posits for suffering and evil a positive role in the salvation process? Let us consider the ways Job and Paul describe their experience of suffering and its meaning.

Job believes that he is a just, righteous, generous man (9:15-16, 20-21; 31:1-40) who has been made to suffer by God (6:4; 7:1-6; 9:17-18; 12:7-10, 14; 16:7-11); he thus experiences God as unjust. The wicked prosper (21:7) while Job is punished, although God knows he is not guilty (10:7-8). In the end, Job has a personal encounter with God that somehow changes his existential situation: now he sees God, while in the past he had only heard of God (42:1-6). Yet Job's agonized question about why the wicked prosper is never given an intellectual answer. His suffering and the unanswered question remain outside of and in conflict with what has been his faith that God justly rewards and punishes in accordance with the quality of one's obedience. Job's existence is somehow sustained by God, but a painful tension remains between his newfound, qualitatively different knowledge of God and his long-held theological belief in the justice of God. There is even in his new faith a tinge of acquiescent resignation to the overwhelming power and mystery of God, and

Job's suffering makes no constructive, harmonious contribution to his new relationship with God.

Paul, unlike Job, has no sense of being subjected to injustice by God. He can portray his life of faith as a continuing unsuccessful effort to do the good that he wills to do (Rom. 7:14-25);[16] even if in another place he can say that he is not aware of anything against himself (that is, has nothing bad on his conscience), he concedes that the Lord may know something that he has pushed down into the dark recesses of his heart (1 Cor. 4:4-5). Paul has renounced confidence in any merit that might attach to his obedience or to his election as a Jew: he has no righteousness of his own, but he does rejoice in the right relationship with God that he has through faith in Christ. And he believes that he has lived out that faith in an appropriate way. He has not reached the goal of full salvation, but he forgets what lies in his past and presses on toward the goal (Phil. 3:7-16). Believing that he has done that well, he feels justified in calling on others to imitate him (1 Cor. 4:16; 11:1; Phil. 3:17).

Paul, like Job, has suffered in carrying out his mission, and he is quite prepared to speak about it graphically. He tells us that he has become a spectacle to all; has been hungry, thirsty, ill-clad, beaten, homeless, weary, reviled, persecuted, slandered (1 Cor. 4:8-13). He has been stoned and shipwrecked; in danger from rivers, bandits, Jews, Gentiles, false brothers and sisters, the city and the wilderness (2 Cor. 11:23-39). The reason Paul does not experience these afflictions as divine injustice is that after his conversion, Paul's central theological conviction is that God has brought radical eschatological salvation through the death and resurrection of Jesus (Rom. 3:21-26; 4:24; 1 Cor. 1:18; 15:3-11). This gives suffering a positive and central place in Paul's faith. Jesus saves by means of his death and resurrection, and those who benefit from this do so by participating in that story: therefore Paul wants to share in Christ's suffering and be conformed to his death, and this is somehow connected to his attaining the resurrection of the dead (Phil. 3:10-11). Paul does not specify the nature of the link between his suffering and his attainment of final salvation, but clearly his suffering is both a means of fellowship with Christ now, and it looks toward his sharing in Jesus' resurrection. He declares that he has been crucified with Christ, and in consequence Christ lives in him (2 Cor. 5:17; compare Gal. 2:19-20). In some texts this death with Christ is internal or existential and occurs by means of sacrament and thoughtful self-interpretation. We have been baptized into Jesus' death, he declares (Rom. 6:3-4), and this frees us from sin (6:5-7). This change is not automatic or magical but must be appropriated by us through the reinterpretation of our lives (6:11). For Paul this entails a radical change of understanding. He no longer believes that his life is grounded on his own ethical performance, but rather on a new relationship with God that God gives by drawing us into faith in Christ, without regard to our moral and religious merit (Phil. 3:7-11). The renunciation of one's self-understanding is a "death" (2 Cor. 5:14-15, 17).

In other texts, however, death and resurrection with Christ is Paul's metaphorical interpretation of his palpable experience of physical, spiritual, and psychological suffering in this public world. Recall

Paul's catalogues of his afflictions. Perhaps most revealing is 2 Cor. 4:7-12, where in four parallel statements he refers to himself as struck down but not destroyed. His afflictions are his participation in the death of Jesus, and his being upheld in his sharing in the resurrected life of Christ. This, however, is not a mystical relationship in the conventional sense of that term but rather a metaphorical one. Paul understands his upset and recovery metaphorically as a new manifestation of Jesus' death and resurrection. Metaphor has the power to draw us into the reality it interprets; thus Paul participates in Christ insofar as he interprets the particulars of his own life anew.

Is it necessary that Paul's attainment of final salvation, resurrection, be mediated by his suffering? Apparently so, in some sense. Always carrying around the death of Jesus in his body has as its purpose (Greek *hina*–"in order that") that the life of Jesus might be manifested in his body (2 Cor. 4:10). Thus the latter (life) is dependent on the former (death) (2 Cor. 4:17). Perhaps we cannot deduce from Paul that the redemptive import of suffering or evil is a universal ontological structure, but Paul's theology does show that it is at least an existential possibility in some cases.

In short, Job experienced his suffering as a contradiction of the normative Jewish faith that he passionately held prior to his suffering. His newfound relationship with God, moreover, has emerged in spite of–not by means of–his suffering. With Paul, on the other hand, there is the closest relation between his experience of suffering and his central theological convictions. His suffering is related to his salvation as the means of his ongoing relationship with the risen Christ. Paul's understanding holds open a redemptive possibility for those who have suffered, in whatever way and from whatever terrors: they can understand that there is a life-affirming reality that is not their own, holding them up when they hit bottom.

Evil and God's Standpoint: Purpose and Result

I have asked whether evil has a necessary relationship to the achievement of God's ultimate purpose, and whether that purpose can confer meaning upon the evil that we suffer. I have considered the theological and existential responses of Job and Paul to their afflictions. But now I want to ask what glimpses the Bible offers, so to speak, of *God's* standpoint.

If humankind and the world were not fallen, obviously God would have no need to use evil persons, acts, or situations to carry out God's life-giving purposes (Gen. 45:5; John 10:10). I accept, however, the biblical witness that we are in fact fallen, and I find very useful Paul Ricoeur's statement of what that means: in every situation in which persons find themselves, evil is always already there.[17] It is already there in the subjectivity of the human heart (Jer. 17:9; Mark 3:5; 6:52; 8:17; 10:5); already there in the conflicts of society (Rom. 1:28-32); already there in the hardness of nature (Gen. 3:14-19). If the biblical God purposes to judge and redeem through and by means of the historical process, in which there are no unflawed human actors, it will be necessary for God to act through troublingly ambiguous agencies.

Isaiah 10:5-14 shows God's action in relation to the *agent* of divine judgment, Assyria. The text does not specifically affirm the *necessity* of this choice, but it is implied. Why, we might ask, was *Assyria in particular* the chosen instrument at just this time? That is really to ask, why did Isaiah interpret the action of Assyria as God's judgment? I offer three possible reasons: (1) Israel needed to be called to account; (2) Assyria was the available nation with the requisite power; (3) God is finally mysterious. We need not suppose that God broke invasively into the historical process or willed for Assyria to be the brutal, arrogant nation that it was: the Isaiah oracle itself condemns Assyria's arrogant violence and disregard for national boundaries. Amos 1-2 gives the same kind of critique of cruel, invasive conquests of one nation by another: Assyria will also get its judgment. Indeed, we may even suppose that eighth-century Judahites reacted to Assyria's cruel invasion in much the same way that Americans responded to 9/11: *We did not deserve such an evil.* Yet Isaiah affirms that God chooses this evil, harmful action as an instrument of judgment, although Assyria has no sense of being God's agent. From the Assyrian standpoint the nation was acting freely, following its own imperialistic intentions, exercising its own conquering power. The broad implication of Isaiah's oracle is that God sometimes carries out God's own purposes in history by using evil human agents, without destroying their limited freedom and autonomy.

In his essay "The Problem of Wonder," Rudolf Bultmann developed this kind of insight into an understanding of God's action in history. For

Bultmann, God's action must be taken seriously as real, but that does not mean subverting the law-abiding, cause-and-effect understanding of history and nature that we as moderns cannot escape. Bultmann distinguishes between miracle and wonder. A miracle—an amazing event, contrary to the orderly sequence of natural events, and demonstrating to sight the action of God—is no longer possible for us to accept. A wonder, on the other hand, is God's action, distinct from the events of the natural world, but it does not demonstrate God to sight, and it can always be understood as an occurrence that accords with natural law. That is to say, wonder is the hidden presence and action of God in the ordinary and is available only to faith, not to sight.[18] In Bultmann's terms, what for Isaiah, was the judgment of Judah at the hand of Assyria was a wonder, not a miracle: that is, we should imagine that the event would have been open to other interpretations.

To take one final, decisive example: in the New Testament, Jesus' death is described as an evil act on the part of those who were most immediately responsible for it. They intended to make him suffer and die. In the Gospel of Mark, Jesus' death is specifically qualified as *necessary* (Greek *dei*: Mark 8:31; see also John 3:14-15; 12:24-25, 32-33). We may ask, "necessary for what?" Mark declares that it was necessary in order for him to fulfill his destiny as determined by Scripture (Mark 9:12; 14:21). But that is a formal, not a material answer, and we must still ask why it was necessary from the standpoint of Scripture for the redeemer to die. Mark does not answer that question directly but suggests that the necessity resides in the situation of those who need to be ransomed (10:45), the beneficiaries of God's action. That is, God chooses an event caused by evil human intentions in order to carry out God's redemptive purpose.

Perhaps Mark's most characteristic expression for the condition of the unredeemed is "hardness of heart" (3:5; 6:52; 8:17; 10:5)—the essential deformation of the wellsprings of will and understanding. For Mark, the overcoming of this hardness of heart requires death. One must be ready to put at risk the *old self*, distorted by a self-regarding hardness of heart—one must take up one's cross and follow Jesus (8:34)—in order to receive anew one's *real self* (8:35). This thought is acheived by a play on two senses of the Greek word *psyche* (soul, that is, self, and life) in 8:35. The self of the hardened heart that one clutches to oneself is lost—risked—to give rise to the real self.

This is a transformation that human beings—the "many" for whom the Son of Man gives his life as a ransom—cannot accomplish on their own (10:27). In order for it to occur it is *necessary* that there be an event that transcends the evil forces of history (10:27), an event in which the many can participate and share, namely, the Son of Man's own move from death to resurrection (Mark. 8:31; 9:31; 10:33-34).

What exactly is the source of the capacity of Jesus' mission to save? The New Testament characteristically puts Jesus' death, his blood (understood eschatologically as a sacrifice), in the dominant position (Mark 14:24; Rom. 3:25; 5:8; 1 Cor. 15:3-4; 2 Cor. 5:4; Gal. 4:4-5; 1 Pet. 1:18-21; Heb. 7:22, 27; 8:13; 9:12, 14-15, 22-23, 26). But we should think that God neither willed Jesus' opponents to kill him nor willed that Jesus should die a violent death in order to carry out his mission. Practicing a moment of deconstructive reflection can lead us to a different understanding.

At a sub-dominant, almost concealed, level, however, the New Testament makes the *obedience* of Jesus' *whole* life, not his sacrificial death, the source of his redeeming power. It was his *obedience* that God willed (Mark 14:36); his violent death was the result of that obedience. Bringing the sub-dominant up to the dominant position offers us another perspective. Jesus' death has a special significance because it is the ultimate expression of his obedience (Rom. 6:9-10). In the context of early Christianity, and in light of the Jewish sacrificial cult, the significance of his death became the dominant interpretation. But we should understand his death as the final expression of the real source of Jesus' saving power—his obedience (Mark 1:11; 14:36)—and not as the source itself. At bottom it is Jesus' obedient righteousness that overcame the consequences of Adam's transgression and led to our justification (Rom 5:18-19). Jesus is the instrument and revelation of God precisely because he obediently makes no claims for himself (John 5:19, 30; 7:16, 28; 8:28, 50; 12:49-50; 14:10, 24). The source of his power is the obedience that he learned through temptation and suffering and that gives an indestructible quality to his whole life (Heb. 3:1, 6; 4:15; 5:7-8; 7:16, 26-28). In Heb. 10:3-20 we see most provocatively an intense struggle between the dominant (sacrifice) and sub-dominant (obedience) interpretations of Jesus mission.

I believe that elevating the sub-dominant interpretation to the dominant level gives us the most satisfactory theological position: The source of

Jesus' power to redeem is Jesus' obedient connection to God, which releases into the stream of history the redemptive power that believers experience as the resurrection of Jesus.

The medium that links Jesus' story with the story of the believer is the word. Jesus' public ministry begins with his preaching of the gospel (Mark 1:14), and very soon people are preaching the word about him (1:45). This is a word that has surprising authority (1:27-28). It spreads, and its power brings hearers thronging to Jesus (1:28, 45; 3:7); this coming Mark interprets as faith (5:27, 34; 10:47, 52), that is, participation in Jesus' story (8:31, 34-37).

Mark interprets Jesus' statement that he gives his life as a ransom (10:45) by juxtaposing immediately to it the story of Jesus' restoring sight to blind Bartimaeus (10:46-52). In Mark, seeing is an image of understanding (4:12; 8:17-18), and understanding is what Jesus has been trying to lead his disciples to (4:13; 8:21; 9:32). Jesus' death as Son of Man focalizes his obedience (14:35-36). And Jesus' obedient death as Son of Man—re-presented in the Gospel's story and interpreted by Jesus' giving of sight /understanding to Bartimaeus—ransoms or liberates by giving the understanding that resides in faith. That the word of the gospel saves by giving understanding is concisely affirmed (Mark 4:13-14, 20, 21-25). Jesus' death, then, saves by being manifested in the word of the whole Gospel narrative. The mission of Jesus meets us in the narrative word that re-presents Jesus' mission to us, a word that has the power to draw us into faith, into participation in Jesus' transformation from death to resurrected life. This is what God has done with the evil deed that Jesus' adversaries committed against him.

My argument in this chapter, based on perspectives found in the Bible itself, is that in a world in which evil is always already present, God, in the mystery of God's inscrutable mind and in God's infinite freedom, sometimes finds it necessary to make use of evil agencies to carry out God's purposes. Those purposes may confer significance upon evil acts, and one such purpose may be the intention of God to enact judgment.

This does not mean that we have a universal philosophical answer to Job's justifiably impatient, appalled, and dismayed question about why the righteous suffer and the wicked prosper (Job 6:4; 7:1-6; 9:15-16; 21:4-7). That question is still painfully present: the reality of the pain should not be diminished, nor should it be assumed when the apparently innocent suffer, they are always only apparently innocent. I have argued from the New Testament that God can turn particular situations of evil into occasions of redemption. By that I do not mean to diminish the gravity of those situations as evil, or to suggest that the redemptive result that God confers upon an evil act—Jesus' crucifixion—necessarily means that the evil intentions of the human actors have a harmonious, logical relationship with God's ultimate purposes, though the redemptive result may have such a relationship.

I earlier cited Walter Brueggemann's understanding of the tension, at the heart of the Old Testament, between its core testimony and its countertestimony. Since these testimonies are in tension regarding what we can expect from God, we for whom the Old Testament is canonical must allow these two traditions to interweave each other. The faith we live out in between them will have its dissonances and uncertainties. To the degree that 9/11 was an evil perpetrated against us, this faith may not be comforting: it may nevertheless be sustaining.

This faith stance allows us to protest what we see in 9/11 as a violation of the justice we have come to expect from a gracious, just, and saving God, while at the same time acknowledging that since we ourselves are not God, we do not have the wisdom or power to question or understand this exception that the mysterious God has made to the justice we expected. This stance also allows us to hope for the ultimate victory of God's now unseen justice, grace, and redemption.[19]

I believe that it would be salutary for the church to assimilate the countertestimony of the Old Testament into its theology, but this should be accompanied by an inseparable admonitory warning. Affirming the countertestimony would give us permission—when we find ourselves in situations of pain, injustice, or chaos that we believe we do not deserve—to voice our feelings. We might say to God: "Why did you let 'the enemy' loose in the world?" Or we might borrow Job's words and accuse God directly: "You have worn me out, shriveled me up, torn and hated me." But we human beings are flagrantly willing, if not eager, to be seduced into self-deception. We are always ready to sell ourselves a favorable cover story in order to conceal the unacceptable real story of our lives. Thus, whenever we are ready to shift the blame on to God, we must at least ask ourselves the question: What is our responsibility for and fault in the situation of evil that engulfs us?

At this point we can grasp how sharp is the paradox of seeing 9/11 as both an evil perpetrated against us and the consequence of evil we have committed as a nation. As an evil done to us, 9/11 is a troubling exception to the justice of God that our tradition has taught us to expect. As judgment of our evil, however, the Old Testament understanding of justice and judgment—action leads to consequence—confers theo-*logical* coherence and consistency upon 9/11. Our action—injustice—leads to consequence—9/11. The witness of the Old Testament is that when the community in its social dealings violates the grace manifested in God's distributive justice, retributive justice legitimately comes into play.

Thus I turn next to address 9/11 as a judgment upon our social injustice.

5.

9/11 and Justice in America: A Hermeneutics of Judgment

Distributive (In)justice in America

We have seen that, in the Old Testament, justice means a preferential concern for the most vulnerable members of society and a push toward reducing the gulf between rich and poor and achieving equality. John Rawls, an extremely important political philosopher of the late twentieth century, has argued convincingly that in a secular, pluralistic democracy, justice must be grounded on the political process and not on theology or metaphysics.[1] However, Rawls's principle of distributive justice maintains a strong continuity with that of the Bible. Goods should be distributed in such a way as to achieve the greatest benefit for the least advantaged, those in the income class with the least expectations. The free and equal citizens of a democratic political community have a right to what they need in order to live a complete life. Inequalities are permitted only when they are made to contribute effectively to the general good or, more exactly, to the least advantaged.[2]

How does America fare when evaluated by this criterion? The following is obviously a selection of economic indicators, but I believe they are none-theless representative in manifesting social injus-tice in our society, the failure to be concerned about the most vulnerable or about the chasm between the rich and the poor. These all have a history that began before the present administration.

↘ During the downsizing outburst of the 1990s, AT&T cut 123,000 jobs; Sears, 50,000; Delta, 18,800; Eastman Kodak, 16,800. Downsizing allows a company to cut costs and tends to cause the price of the company's stock to go up. Some-times it is necessary for financial reasons, but in other cases it is done to increase the profits of an already profitable company. For example, early in its downsizing process (1998) Eastman had had a 9% increase in earnings.[3] ↘ In the United States, some 40 million people are without health insur-ance. At the same time, the three largest annual salaries of CEOs at HMOs in 1997 were $30.7 mil-lion, $12.4 million, and $8.6 million. The U.S. spends a greater percentage of its gross domestic product on health care than any other country in the world.[4] ↘ Among developed nations, the U.S. spends the lowest percentage of its gross domes-tic product on social security: 11.5% as compared with over 20% in Belgium, the Netherlands, France and Sweden.[5] ↘ In 1974, the ratio of the typical CEO's salary to the average workers' salary was

35:1. By the 1990s, it had risen to 120:1. The figure cited in 1999 was 419:1.[6] → In 1989, 12.8% of the population lived below the poverty line, and by 1992, 18% of full time workers were below the poverty line. Twenty million people suffer from malnutrition. Among industrialized countries, the U.S. has the highest poverty rates.[7] → The distance between the incomes of the highest 20% and the lowest 20% in the U.S. is greater than in any other industrialized country.[8]

Our leaders speak publicly a great deal about the freedom that we enjoy in this country and want to export to others, but rarely do we critically ask who should be the primary beneficiaries of economic freedom. The question can be put in different ways. Given realistic limits to economic growth, can we allow unconstrained freedom for individual gain and for the already affluent to increase their prosperity, or should the freedom of this relatively small group of individuals be limited in order to enhance the free access of the many to meet their needs?[9] Should not the least advantaged be enabled to live in modest comfort, to have wealth and income sufficient to reach a wide range of goals and to be afforded the social basis for a sense of self-worth?[10] Or, to put the question another way, should we support the drive to acquire possessions and guarantee virtually unlimited freedom of choice and preference primarily for the well off? Should we afford them the opportunity to select their favorites from as wide a variety as possible of available products and brands of consumer goods? Or should we support the goal of guaranteeing the basic necessities of life to the majority of the world's people, who out of economic necessity lack the freedom to participate in the consumer project?[11]

It is obvious, from the magnitude of the American population who live in poverty and without health insurance, who work at more than one job but still can hardly survive, that over the decades we have given priority to the freedom of the relatively few individuals to acquire enormous wealth and to spend it lavishly on an elaborate variety of consumer luxuries.

We have seen that in the Old Testament, such disparities are the results of injustice, and injustice calls down divine judgment. Justice means, domestically, that everyone should have land and resources sufficient to participate in community life, and internationally, that one nation should not violate the land and integrity of other nations. Given the examples just considered of pervasive social injustice, can the United States be seen as a seriously unjust society—and thus as subject to divine judgment?

Resistance to Interpreting 9/11 as Judgment

Public commentary on 9/11 has largely avoided or resisted interpreting that day's events as divine judgment. I am sure that I have only scratched the surface of the large volume of sermons preached to address 9/11, but I have read some fifty,[12] and the themes running through them are remarkably consistent: There is a noticeable stress on the evil perpetrated against an innocent, or at least undeserving, America, and appeals are made to trust in the God of the future. Comfort is offered in the face of undeserved suffering. Some sermons recognize the need for America to repent and to avoid taking vengeance, but I see a general reluctance to regard 9/11 as the deserved judgment of God, as well as fervent, explicit denials that it could possibly be so understood. I have found a few nuanced probings toward such an interpretation; but *only one* fully articulated argument that 9/11 should be understood as judgment upon our nation for its social injustice and imperialism, and upon the church for its failure to distinguish Christian faith from American patriotism.[13]

I understand that reluctance. In the face of the suffering and devastation experienced on that fateful day, comfort was urgently needed and altogether appropriate. In sermons preached soon after the event, I understand why the theme of judgment would be very much muted. It is more troubling, however, when a respected social ethicist like Jean Bethke Elshtain argues strongly from her considered, critical judgment that there are only two possible interpretations of the event: *either* 9/11 was an "unspeakable horror" (says Pope John Paul II), *or* it was a "glorious deed" (says Osama bin Laden). Elshtain vehemently denies that 9/11 can be seen as judgment upon us because, she says, in no way do "we" (meaning either the people or the nation) deserve judgment. It would be especially wrong, she argues, both morally and practically, to blame 9/11 on the things our national government has done (that is, foreign policy). Islamist fundamentalists attack us, she declares, not for what we have done, but because of what we are: a free and pluralistic society, having personal and civic liberties grounded in our Constitution. We must and will fight, not to conquer countries or destroy peoples, but to defend who we are and what we represent at our best.[14]

One wonders how Elshtain so completely missed both the Old Testament critique of injustice and important aspects of the present state of American society like those I have outlined above. She has insisted, to the contrary, that 9/11 be understood solely as evil perpetrated against us.

One other interpreter has raised pointed questions that bear consideration here. Jon P. Gunnemann also rejects the judgment interpretation of 9/11, but with some acknowledgment of American guilt, and from a perspective different from Elshtain's.[15] He maintains that to interpret this event as God's judgment would require that we treat all human misfortunes in the same way, and thus we would trivialize human suffering and render God capricious. I do not believe that those claims stand up. I take the suffering visited upon us very seriously, as the previous chapter demonstrates. My interpretation does not make God capricious, for I see God's judging action as strongly motivated by God's demand for righteousness and justice (as in the Old Testament prophets). This does not mean that I interpret *all* human misfortunes as eschatological judgment. The events of 9/11 have some distinguishing characteristics that have conferred upon the day an extraordinary magnitude: (1) It has attracted a wide array of interpretations, and this makes it analogous to Old Testament prophetic oracles in which events are seen as judgment—or approval—in light of the prophet's interpretive vision. (2) 9/11 has taken on the character of a kairotic moment, a time-defining event: that is, for the American collective consciousness, and especially in the propaganda of the Bush administration, it has become the crucial event that divides our national historical time into a "before" and an "after." (3) The Bush administration has used this interpretation to justify an immense domestic and foreign policy agenda that many severely question.

Why do Elshtain and others insist upon, or fall into, a partial, one-dimensional interpretation of 9/11? I suggest that it is because we human beings tend to resist having conflicting, clashing thoughts and feelings about the phenomena that encounter us in the world. Therefore, when we are faced with something that threatens us with such painful ambivalence and dissonance, we seek to escape that dissonance by reducing the complexity of the phenomenon in order to comprehend it in a unified and harmonious way. I am not arguing that we should understand 9/11 exclusively as judgment, but that we should summon the nerve to accept the dissonant perception that it may have been *both* judgment upon us *and* an unjust evil perpetrated against us. I do not mean to minimize the evil of the perpetrators of these attacks: as we have seen, to perceive a wicked nation or group as the instrument of divine judgment is consistent with oracles in the major Old Testament prophets. At the same time that Isaiah regarded both Assyria and Babylon as instruments of God's judgment, he also accused them of arrogance, cruelty, and greed and held them subject to that same judgment (Isa. 10:5-12; 14:3-20).

Looking Forward, Looking Back

One other aspect of the biblical understanding of judgment offers a helpful lens for grasping the significance of 9/11. We may distinguish between *prospective* and *retrospective* proclamations of judgment. The Tower of Babel story looks back upon a past event of judgment: The people sought to build a city and tower that would elevate them to divine power and status, but God terminated the venture before it could succeed. The prophets, on the other hand, regularly look forward, predicting a future act of divine judgment (Isa. 1:24; 5:5-6, 8-9; 10:1-11; Hos. 13:7-11; Amos 2:13-16; 3:15; 6:8-14). However, the prophets also look back on past events of judgment (Isa. 1:7-8; 9:8-21; Hos. 6:4-5; Amos 4:6-13), and project into the future an aspect of Israel's past history with God. We could say that from the prophet's standpoint, Israel is always standing between judgments. Israel faces judgment in the future because it has not heeded and responded to judgments in the past. The past is a warning about the future.

Similarly, in the Tower of Siloam episode (Luke 13:1-5) Jesus looks back on a past event. As we have seen, he denies that the victims were being punished for their sins, but implies that his audience is sinful (Otherwise why would he summon them to repentance: "If you do not repent, you will all perish as the eighteen did"?) Here as well, a past destructive event is seen as a warning to repent, that is, to act in the present so as to avoid another calamity in the future. The warning illumines the present as a time that presses one to repent. In this case, Jesus declines to interpret a past calamity as divine judgment for sin, but nevertheless projects the possibility of a future judgment—unless his audience repents. As we saw with regard to the Old Testament prophets, we need not read this future judgment as an extraneous intervention into the present: because Jesus makes the future judgment contingent upon whether or not the people repent, we may consider the judgment of which he speaks as a working out of an intrinsic disintegrative process. Repentance, then, would mean acting so as to reverse the social decay arising from injustice.

Further, as in the case of the Old Testament prophets, it is Jesus' interpretive word that makes the fall of the tower a crucial and demanding occurrence for his audience. It takes both event and word to make the event arresting. Without Jesus' provocative questions, his audience would perhaps have been existentially disengaged from the past event, with no interest in it beyond the abstract question about the degree of sin on the part of someone else—the victims. It is through the power of Jesus' word that the fall of the tower becomes an event for the audience, to move and challenge them. Without that word, the event is theologically mute.

The same is true, I suggest, for the events of 9/11.

I hasten to add that this dual perspective, looking backward as well as forward, means that in the biblical understanding, the occasion of judgment is also an opportunity to move toward redemption (for example, Isa. 1:18-20, 24-28; 2:2-4; 5:5-6; 10:20-22; 30:19; Hos. 13:7-10; Amos 3:15; 6:8-14). The fall of Samaria and, later, of Jerusa-

lem were seen as fulfilling prophecies of a ruinous future (Jer. 21:3-10; 23:1-4; 29:10-11; 34:2);
but, writing later, the Second Isaiah maintained
that the time of punishment was over and that
God was ready to begin a new redemptive thing
(Isa. 40:1-11; 51:4-11). The people's response to
this new possibility was mixed, however: some
responded in faithfulness, but others did not and
so were faced with another destructive Day of the
Lord (Zech. 13:2, 8; 14:1-3; Mal. 4:1, 5). Seen over
the historical long run, the prophetic perspective
indicates that if warning events of the past are
not seen as creating moments of decision, if the
people do not respond in a radical enough way
to change the present situation, then another Day
always impends from the future.

We see something similar in the Gospel of John,
where the import of judgment/crisis (Greek *krisis*) is similar to the pressure to repent in Luke's
story of the Tower of Siloam. The Gospel plays on
the nouns *krisis* and *krima*, and the verb *krin-
ein*, which bear both the connotations "crisis" and
"condemnation." In John 3:19 John declares, "This
is the *krisis*," with the connation *crisis*, meaning
an event that presents people with an inescapable
decision. Jesus appears in the world as the light
of truth and understanding (1:3-5; 8:12; 9:5), and
his appearance requires that people decide either
to come to the light or reject it (3:19-21; 6:60-
71). Those who come to the light, believing, are
willing to be exposed for what they are, and are
not condemned (3:18), but those who refuse the
light because their deeds are evil are condemned
already (3:18). The *future* judgment has become
a *present* reality for them because, having rejected

the saving light, they remain in the blindness of untruth and misunderstanding (9:39-41). John's understanding of "crisis" accords with Sissela Bok's definition, in a splendid book on lying: a crisis is "a turning point at which a decisive change for better or worse may take place."[16] Judgment, as the Gospel understands it, is neither the end of the cosmos nor of the nation, but of our personal life-worlds, and thus is an important moment in coming to moral and religious maturity.

What kind of turning point—if any—will 9/11 be for America?

What we have seen of biblical perspectives on divine judgment allows us to consider that question in both prospective and retrospective ways. If we envision 9/11 through the lens of the Tower of Siloam, it is a warning to change the present in order to escape a destructive future. If we view it through the lens of John's understanding of crisis, a failure to make the right response in the face of a call to decision will already have condemned us to an ever-worsening inability to recognize the truth of our condition and to act on that truth. On the other hand, if we view 9/11 in the light of the Tower of Babel and certain prophetic texts, we may regard the event retrospectively as retribution and punishment for our arrogance and injustice.

Justifications for Interpreting 9/11 as Judgment

Can, and should, Christian theology still regard certain past events as retributive judgment? I discussed the *logical* connection between distributive

and retributive justice in Chapter 2; now my interest is more particularly in concrete reasons why
I believe the theme of divine judgment, which
appears so prominent in the biblical materials,
provides at least a possible hermeneutical lens for
understanding 9/11. I contend that the judgment
theme is indispensable to a biblical Christian theology because such a theology thinks about God
and history together, and because the biblical God
demands justice.

I reiterate that by "divine judgment" I do not
mean a divine invasive movement "from above"
that interrupts the normal flow of human history; I
mean rather an event, resulting from human interests and motives belonging to this world, in which
God's action is completely hidden, but which the
believing community interprets as a divine action,
though it is always open to other interpretations.
Recall that in the Bible, judgment has two essential
and inseparable aspects: an event, which has happened or is expected to happen, and the prophet's
interpretive word, into which the event is taken up
so as to become a word-event. The event of judgment so conceived is a focalized instance of God's
secret or hidden action.

There are three reasons why the theme of judgment, applied retrospectively or prospectively, is
indispensable if biblical theology is to maintain
its integrity.

1. The proclamation of judgment undergirds the
inherent significance and prominence of justice in
the Bible's view of God's created order: it sanctions God's demand for justice by offering a for-
ward-looking reason to obey; and it holds human
beings accountable.

To deny that a catastrophic event like 9/11, occurring in a context of American injustice (including both domestic and foreign policy), could properly be interpreted as judgment is to depreciate the value and significance of justice for human life and to diminish the reality of the divine command that justice should prevail. Denying that judgment happens deprives God's demand for justice of an important sanction. Judgment, expressed as punishment, sanctions and enforces the demand of distributive justice, and it carries out the equalizing function that is the proper business of retributive justice. One who has gained too much loses something while one who has lost too much gains something.

Yet responding positively to the sanction—doing righteousness in order to avoid punishment—is the external form of a more internal, existential movement. As Rudolf Bultmann long ago reminded us,[17] in what a person *does*, his or her real *being, the self that he or she is to become*, is at stake. In deciding to obey God in order to receive reward and avoid punishment, one is deciding who one *will be*. To attain oneself is a legitimate intention of ethical behavior. The paradox to which Bultmann pointed is that one surrenders to God in order to arrive at oneself (see Luke 17:33). The reward is, finally, attaining the (individual or national) self that God intends. Of course, in the decision *not* to obey, the self is also at stake, and what one finally arrives at, in Johannine terms, is the deterioration of the ability to recognize and act on the truth.

2. The proclamation of judgment gives a sharp and much needed wake-up call to a humanity that is morally deaf, blind, and obdurate.

In the prophetic tradition, the event of retributive judgment—in concrete terms, foreign invasion and destruction—is described as enormous, overwhelming, riveting, capturing the attention in an inescapable and preternatural way. I referred to this earlier as the prophets' "electric language." This heightened style speaks to the way some of the most incisive biblical witnesses describe the human condition. For example, Israel is led astray by a victimizing spirit of whoredom and is unable to return (Hos. 4:12; 5:4); the human heart is devious and perverse beyond understanding (Jer. 17:9), or in Ezekiel's words (11:19-20), we have in our flesh a heart of stone. We lack the power to do the good we will to do (Rom. 7:18-19), and we are incapable of truth because we are under a demonic power whose nature is lying (John 8:43-47). If we as human beings really are that obdurately hardened against truth and righteousness, it will take a bugle blast, an *explosive* event, to function as a wake-up call. 9/11 was certainly explosive. Only time will tell which way we move: whether into the light, or deeper into darkness.

In a lecture about her own fiction, short-story writer and novelist Flannery O'Connor once stated that she used violence (read: "electric language") in her stories because only violence was capable of returning her characters to reality and preparing them to accept their moment of grace. Their heads were so hard that almost nothing else will do the work. This idea, that we can be returned to reality only at considerable cost, is seldom understood by the casual reader, but is implicit in the Christian view of the world:[18] from a biblical point of view, when O'Connor spoke these words, she was thinking God's thoughts.

3. The proclamation of judgment gives coherence, completeness, and meaning to the story-like character of individual and corporate human existence. The refusal to acknowledge judgment denies that human beings are accountable: it assumes that we can violate the moral demands of the covenant, and it will not cost us anything. This assumption rejects the prominent biblical belief that actions have consequences. But that biblical belief informs the merging of meaningful content and the chronological succession of events that characterizes biblical narrative. Biblical narrative flows forward through time (1) from possibility (beginning), (2) through intention to act and action (middle), (3) to consequence (end). The fundamental biblical narrative plot of individual and national existence is cut short when it is deprived of its ending, that is, judgment. The biblical story just fizzles out; or changing the metaphor, the flowing river of biblical narrative loses its channel, and its water is dissipated into the chaos of the swamp. Such a loss subverts the historicity of existence; it undercuts the biblical claim that we move toward *something*; we become who we are, through the connected process of our decisions and their consequences.

It is theologically important and salutary to understand 9/11 as judgment, as the consequence or end of one part of our national story. It is salutary because, as I showed above, judgment, from the biblical point of view, is always an occasion to move into redemption: to see it as end is to be able to see it also as a new beginning. To envision a segment of our past as a whole three-part plot gives order and coherence to what would otherwise be a chaotic sequence of "one damn thing after another."

It also opens up the beginning of a new story, as we see in the Gospel narratives themselves: the Gospels end with both the death (termination) and the resurrection (new beginning) of Jesus.

Given the Bible's view of human sin, it is hard to see how the good news could come to expression in any other way than through the ending that is judgment. It is *necessary* for the old to die in order for the new to be born (Hos. 6:1-3; Ezek. 37:1-14). It was necessary for the Son of Man to suffer and die in order to be raised and to become the ransom for the many (Mark 8:31; 10:45), and those who are redeemed will also be drawn into this sequence, from old to new, from the death of the old person or community (or, in the Old Testament, of the old nation) to the birth of the new (Mark 8:34-37; Rom. 6:1-11; 1 Cor. 15:20-24; 2 Cor. 5:14-15, 17; John 12:24-26, 32). Only the radicalness of a "death" can undo the fixedness of the old. Without judgment as a "death" that breaks up the demonic structure of the old, which imprisons us, there can be no new beginning of life. Thus it is theologically important, even necessary, to maintain the reality of judgment as a consequent event. Given the human condition, retributive judgment is the dark side of a redemptive event, without which there can be no redemption.

In his 1959 novel *Set This House on Fire*, William Styron, despite his claims to have outgrown Christianity, showed how much his vision had in fact been shaped by the Bible. The aging father of the novel's narrator turns out to have a prophetic voice. He declares to his son:

Peter, these are miserable times . . . empty times . . . mediocre times. . . . You can almost sniff the rot in the air. And what is more, they are going to get worse. . . . Sometimes I think this is just a nation of children . . . of childish little minds. . . . What this great land of ours needs is something to happen to it. . . . Something ferocious and tragic, like what happened to Jericho—something terrible I mean, son, so that when the people have been through hell-fire and the crucible, and have suffered agony enough and grief, they'll be men again, human beings, not a bunch of smug contented hogs rooting at the trough. . . . We've got to start from scratch again, build from the ground floor up. What has happened to this country would shame the Roman Empire at its lowest ebb. . . . The common man he had his belly stuffed. . . . He hadn't grown in dignity or wisdom. . . . He forswore his Creator, paying this kind of nasty mealy-mouthed lip service every Sunday to the true God while worshiping with all his heart nothing but the almighty dollar.[19]

I wish to contrast the perspective of this fictitious, aging Virginia "liberal" and that of the actual members of the Project for the New American Century (later the Bush cabal). The former believes something terrible needs to happen to us *in order to reestablish our humanity*. The latter wanted a "new Pearl Harbor" *in order to justify the expansion of imperialistic domination of the world*. It is the former, I contend, that expresses one aspect of the biblical understanding of judgment.

Doubts about the Judgment Interpretation

Though I contend that we should understand 9/11 as an event of judgment, I also believe we should be tentative and hesitant in making that assertion. We properly stand back from it at the same time that we make it, for at least two reasons. The first reason is that human beings cannot penetrate the mystery of God. As we have seen, even Jesus declined to interpret the fall of the Tower of Siloam retrospectively as a judgment for sin upon those who died (although he did, at the same time, contemplate a possible prospective judgment awaiting his audience). God would be mysterious even if human beings were not flawed, but our self-interest and self-deception only render our discernment even more problematic. In Matt. 7:1-5, Jesus sternly admonishes his audience not to judge others, first, prudentially, to avoid having the same judgment turned back against you; but second, because none of us can render an accurate judgment. It is not just that my fault as a potential judge is worse than the fault of the person I would judge, but also that I am so self-deceived that I *do not notice* that fault; my powers of discernment are so deformed that I cannot judge truly and helpfully. Jesus' words here (7:1-5) suggest that only after I have self-critically cleared up my own blindness may I be helpfully critical of another; only then may I be able to judge well.

The ambiguity, generated by both the mysterious dimension of God's dealings and uncertainty about our capacity to transcend self-deception based on self-interest, cautions hesitation about

making negative judgments ourselves or interpreting public events as God's judgment. But how
much hesitation?

The second reason for standing back cautiously
from interpreting 9/11 as God's judgment has to do
with the nature of metaphor. When I discuss those
events as divine judgment by viewing them in the
light of—seeing them *as*—the Tower of Babel, or
Isaiah's song of the vineyard (5:1-6), or his oracle
against Samaria, a city with a tower (9:8-12 LXX),
I am placing 9/11 in a metaphorical structure. I
am suggesting that the damage to America is to
be seen as *judgment* just as were the termination
of the building of Babel, the ravaging of Samaria
(which the people arrogantly say they will rebuild),
or the devastation of the diligently cultivated vineyard (Israel and Judah) that has produced only wild
grapes (that is, injustice: 5:7). In each of these
images we have an actor, God, and an action that
God performs—terminating, ravaging, devastating.
In effect, we have the transcendent and holy God
represented as a wrecking crew.

Paul Ricoeur contended that the primary defining feature of metaphor is that it predicates of a
term from one semantic field (the transcendent
God, for example) a meaning from another very
different field of meaning (wrecking a city). One
thing is seen *as* another, quite unexpected thing,
thus creating ambiguity and semantic tension.[20]
The puzzling, less well-know subject—for example,
the kingdom of God, in Jesus' teaching—is seen as
something more familiar—a woman hiding leaven
in flour (Matt. 13:33).

When I choose to interpret 9/11 as judgment,
I am creating a metaphorical connection between

those events and some of the Old Testament metaphors of judgment. What is it about the specifically
metaphorical nature of the judgment interpretation
that inclines us to some degree of reticence about
this interpretation? Again I follow Ricoeur,[21] who
sees three tensions at work in metaphorical utterance. First, the metaphor results from the tension
between two terms in the utterance: in our case,
transcendent God and the wrecking crew. Second,
the metaphor resides in the tension between two
interpretations of the utterance. The *literal* interpretation self-destructs because it is absurd or contradictory in light of the ordinary, conventional
meanings of the subject and the modifier ("wreck-
ing/transcendent God"); this failure of the literal
interpretation opens up the way for a new, metaphorical interpretation based on a suspension of
those conventional meanings. The metaphor may
now refer to a world of new existential possibilities,
a redescription of the world, a new way of being in
the world. The third tension Ricoeur discusses has
to do with the nature or status of the new existential project that is imaged in the metaphor. What
kind of being does the redescribed world have that
is given to us in the metaphor?

The metaphor does not tell us literally what the
new world *is* but rather what it *is like*. The "is like"
embodies a tension-laden "is" and "is not," both
of which must be maintained. The death of the old
and birth of the new contained in judgment both is
and is not given in the metaphor.

The yes and no of the metaphor's reference to
the new world create some ambiguity in our *perception* of what is referred to, and this casts some
ambiguity over the status-in-reality of *what is*

perceived—the new beginning waiting in the ending of the old. The "isness" of the new possibility, however, is real even though our perception of it is not total, and the metaphor has the potential power to draw us into participation in the reality it discloses.

Is 9/11, then, the eschatological judgment of America? Well, yes and no. But, more precisely, I maintain a qualified *yes*. The considerations that I have entertained that count against the judgment interpretation caution us against undue certainty about this position. They lack the force, however, to override the powerful constellation of factors—social, political, moral, logical, existential, and theological—that sustain the judgment interpretation.

Part Two

What Have We Been Doing?
Where Might We Be Headed?

6.

Introduction: In Between Warning and Disaster

I have structured the following chapters according to the understanding of the human situation in history that we see in concentrated miniature in The Tower of Siloam story, in the Synoptic Gospel tradition broadly, within certain prophetic books, and in the prophetic view of history that unfolds in a series of prophets (see Chapter 5). We stand in between warning events of the past—characteristically disregarded—and possibly devastating consequences impending in the future.

To regard such possible future consequences as divine judgment is, obviously, an interpretative theological claim. While no interpretive appraisal of human affairs provides us with certainty, I seek to present a picture of the public posture of the United States—domestic and international—that is broad enough to make such an interpretation plausible. While my own conceptual horizon is theological, in the following pages I will emphasize the insights of perceptive contemporary thinkers who—quite apart from theological considerations—discern incipient, developing ruin in our present course

This theo-historical perspective prompts three questions. (1) What have we been doing since a 9/11? Have we heard the warning to change? (2) Where might we be headed? What kinds of disasters might erupt—or emerge almost unnoticed—from our continuing in the same tracks? (3) What changes should we make to avoid catastrophe? What new directions should we take in order to achieve justice and, hopefully, turn aside an unwanted ending? If we, as Christians, maintain the biblical affirmation that God wills the good for humankind, then we have an obligation to support measures to restore and sustain life from whatever sources these measures arise.

Recall that biblical justice contains both specific rules—like the requirement of honesty in the marketplace and fairness before the judge's bench—and also broad principles: namely, that God intends that all human creatures should have life and well-being, that all people should have their basic needs met and have enough wealth to participate in the community's life. That requires that we should always be in the process of reducing the gap between rich and poor. In order to apply biblical justice to our current situation, we must determine what constitutes life and resources sufficient to participate in community life according to the character of our present culture. Violation of either the rules or the principles constitutes injustice. Recall as well that the Bible assumes that this understanding of justice is accessible to and understandable by all human beings, and that all are accountable to God for its enactment.

The following chapters distinguish between domestic affairs and foreign affairs, and, with regard to domestic affairs, between justice issues for which the American people are largely responsible and those for which the government bears primary responsibility. These distinctions, however, cannot be neatly maintained. When I speak of policies and practices for which the people are responsible, I do not necessarily mean that these have no government involvement, but that Americans have long seemed willing to accept them without significant resistance. Finally, there are many more topics of importance than I can take up here, and thus my discussion will have to be selective, illustrative, and abbreviated.

7.

What Have We Been Doing Since 9/11? Domestic Affairs

Have we heard the warning? Perhaps in some ways we have, but there are many failures that are broad, deep and troubling. Remember the story of the Tower of Siloam. Were those on whom it fell more guilty than those who were spared? Jesus refused to say, but he told his listeners to heed the calamity as a warning to change lest they, too, perish. And remember Flannery O'Connor's words about how violently one must speak to show people how hard and costly it is to be returned from existential death to reality and life.

Was 9/11 a sufficiently forceful warning to us to change? At this point there is much to suggest that it was not. So what *have* we been doing?

The aftermath of hurricane Katrina is a telling display of several interwoven threads of injustice in which both the American people and the government were complicit. It reveals the compounded results of an economic system that generates a large population of poor people, the racism that imposes an excessive proportion of that poverty on African Americans, the incompetence of an administration founded on cronyism, and a hurricane that was intensified by the overheated water of the Gulf of Mexico, one result of the extravagant carbon emissions that flow from our ever-expanding consumer culture. Katrina suggests some of what we have continued to do since 9/11. But the full picture of our complicity in injustice is much broader.

Our Shared Responsibility

→ **Health Care.** There are still some 41 million Americans without health insurance. A survey by the Institute of Medicine found that 18,000 Americans die every year because they have no health insurance.[1] Health care has not improved since 9/11, due in significant part to the power of corporations to prevent change. The Business Roundtable, composed of the leading corporate CEOs, has acquired considerable power to influence economic and political policy, and had substantial effect on the 1994 health care debate.[2] When the Clinton administration proposed reforms that actually seemed designed, on balance, to protect the drug and insurance companies, the latter mounted crushing opposition to even its modest changes.

Americans pay more when they get sick than do the people of any other Western country, and they receive poorer care. In 2002, the U.S. spent $5,267 per person on health care; Canada spent $2,931; Germany, $2,817; and Britain, $2,160. Yet we have a lower life expectancy and higher infant mortality rate than any of these other countries. A survey of nearly 7,000 sick adults in the U.S., Australia, Canada, New Zealand, Britain, and Germany showed that Americans were the most likely to have at least $1,000 in out-of-pocket expenses. More than a half went without needed care because of the cost, and 34% reported being the victim of medical errors such as wrong medications, incorrect test results, and mistaken treatment. The incidence of such reported errors was 30% in Canada, 27% in Australia, 25% in New Zealand, 23% in Germany, and 22% in Britain. Some suggest that the reason for the excessive costs in the U.S. is the administrative bureaucracy required to minimize the payment of health care claims.[3]

The moral import of these conditions is that we treat health care as a privilege rather than a right. There is no moral reason why people living in poverty should have less access to good health care than people living in wealth, however. Neither is our present system necessary for economic efficiency. Michael Lerner projects that a 2% increase in the income tax would cover all the expenses of a universal public health care system, would be cheaper than the present system, and could still leave the administration and delivery of care to the private sector.[4]

→ **The Rich and the Poor.** In America the relative positions of the rich and the poor are determined by the working of "free-market" capitalism, whose system can be described—very summarily—in terms of the following constituent elements. (1) The basic rules of corporate operation are that the company must show a profit over time, and must grow and expand. Profit is the ultimate measure of all corporate decisions, taking precedence over community well-being, worker health, and environmental protection. It is assumed that actions that yield the greatest financial return to corporate stockholders will also be the most beneficial for society: The benefits will trickle down. (2) Competition can be counted on to control supply and demand and ensure the efficient allocation of resources. (3) The negative corollary is that the freedom of the "free" market requires an arena that is free from government regulation and intervention. Regulations to protect workers' safety, prevent worker exploitation, or protect the environment are to be resisted. The use of the tax system or any other measure to manage the economy in order to achieve a more equitable income distribution is also strongly opposed. All such regulations and interventions are held to be "in restraint of trade." (4) Private property is the absolute and exclusive possession of the owner, who has the right to bar others from its use. Whatever the owner does not consume for immediate human needs can be used as capital to accumulate more wealth. Though these seem almost unquestionable truisms today, from a moral point of view exclusive property—"It's your money"—is incompatible with the idea that the general populace has a *right* to well-being.

In free-market capitalism, those with money are positioned to get more, by lending it for interest or investing it or starting a business, and their lives improve. The middle class can hardly do this. In 2004, more than half of American households owned no stock at all, and two-thirds of those that did held portfolios valued at less than $5,000. They have very little wealth outside of their homes. It is much worse for the really poor—those without money—who are positioned to get even less, and their lives decline further. For them, every problem turns into a crisis. Consider a mother earning low wages, who cannot afford professional help for her disabled child and at times must stay at home to care for her. As a result, she loses her job and must take one that pays even less, if she can find one at all.

In American capitalism, the rich get richer and the poor poorer, as the gulf between them widens. This conclusion is not simply an abstract possibility drawn from the nature of the system but is what has actually happened in our recent history. From the 1920s to the early 1970s, unionized blue-collar jobs lifted tens of millions of working Americans into the middle class. Yet in the manufacturing companies of that era, the ratio of CEO pay to median production worker's pay ranged from 25:1 to 40:1. The chief casualty of the new economic regime has been the loss of the blue-collar middle class.[6] In the years between 1966 and 2001, the rise in wages and salaries in the middle of the income distribution was 11%, while the rise at the top of the income distribution was 617%. This does not include investment income, demonstrating that the dramatic increase in the earnings of the very richest has not been due to income from their shrewd investments but to their growing share of income from labor. The most important element in the increase in our general, broad-based prosperity has been the increase in the productivity of our workers, yet unfairly, the lion's share of the increased wealth generated by increased productivity has gone to corporate profits and management pay, while the workers who are in large part responsible for the increased productivity have seen pitiful pay increases and have lost such benefits as guaranteed pensions because these are regarded as an unacceptable drag on profits.[7]

By 2004, the best-off had wealth amounting to 190 times that of a typical household.[8] In mid-2005, for the first time since measurement began, household incomes failed to increase for five straight years.[9] In January 2006, inflation rose at the fastest pace in four months but workers' average weekly earnings, adjusted for inflation, dropped by 0.4% as compared with January 2005.[10] CEOs, however, did better: According to a survey of 550 companies, their median pay rose 11.3% in 2005. The ratio of the pay of the average CEO at a Standard & Poor's 500 firm to the pay of the average U.S. worker currently stands at 430:1.[11]

In his 2005 book, *God's Politics*, Jim Wallis reported that the poverty rate had increased over the three previous years; one of six children in America is poor (13 million); 36 million live below the poverty line; 4 million families are hungry; 14 million have housing needs. The poverty line has not been adjusted in forty years: in 2003 it stood at $18,810 for a family of four.[12] The magnitude of poverty notwithstanding, the corporate world meanwhile pursues its relentless quest for profit: The oil companies defended their huge profits in 2005 ($32.8 billion in earnings for the third quarter) and multi-million dollar bonuses to executives while consumers paid $3 per gallon at the pump.[13] As Delphi headed into bankruptcy and asked for big sacrifices from workers, top management stood to reap large benefits.[14] Pharmaceutical giant Merck suppressed evidence regarding the heart attack danger from its product Vioxx despite claiming it had disclosed all the evidence.[15]

It is no wonder, as Paul Krugman reports, that this is an age of anxiety for the American worker. The corporate order itself, which used to guarantee its workers job security, health care, and a dignified retirement, no longer has the stability and capacity to make such guarantees.[16]

In a 2006 speech, Bill Moyers declared that the majority of Americans "may" support affordable health care, decent wages, safe working conditions, good education, and clean air and water for all, but the government is not delivering.[17] Is Moyers right that this is what the majority of the American people "may" want? Do we—really?

Government Responsibility for Fiscal Policy

→ The Living Wage. At $5.15 per hour, working forty hours per week, fifty-two weeks per year, a minimum wage earner would make $10,700 annually—about $6,000 less than the federal poverty line for a family of three. The U.S. Congress has recently rejected the opportunity to raise the federal minimum to $7.25 an hour, though 83% of Americans would favor an increase. The chief argument against an increase is that it would prompt employers to hire fewer people and thus would hurt the people it should help. That has not happened, however, in states that have raised the minimum wage, and in 2004 more than five hundred economists, including four Nobel laureates in economics, endorsed the idea of valuing work by establishing a wage floor beneath which employers may not pay workers.[18]

Only about 3% of those in the workforce are actually paid at or below the minimum wage of $5.15 per hour. Most low-wage workers start at $6.50 to $7.50 an hour, but even this provides an annual income that is below the federal poverty line for a family of four. While other costs—like housing—must be considered in trying to solve the poverty problem, a living wage establishes a standard of decency with regard to work.[19] The living-wage movement believes that universal wage fairness can be established only through legislative action by the U.S. Congress, especially legislation indexed to inflation. This has not happened, but there have been some 34 successes at the local level, the most notable in Santa Fe, New Mexico, where in January 2006 the minimum wage was raised to $9.50 per hour, the highest rate in the U.S. The immediate goal of the movement is to put the issue on the ballot in several states.[20]

As the Santa Fe City Council engaged in appropriate planning and consultations, critics objected that instituting a city minimum wage higher than the federal one would put Santa Fe at a disadvantage in relation to other nearby cities that paid less, and would violate "free-market" principles against government interference in business. As the discussion proceeded, however, the living-wage proponents put forward moral arguments that they discovered were often more effective than economic ones, contending that it is unjust to expect people to work for less than they can live on. Minimally decent employment trumps an absolutely free market. The Santa Fe City Council passed an ordinance on February 26, 2003, establishing a minimum wage of $8.50, which was to rise to $9.50 in 2006 and $10.50 in 2008. The city was sued by a group of employers who felt that they suffered negative consequences, but the city's policy was upheld by the courts.[21]

There were some very positive results. A number of employers reported that they did not lose customers despite raising prices 1% to 3% to cover their increased labor costs. The city's employment picture remained healthy, with overall employment increasing. The number of families in need of temporary assistance declined significantly.[22]

⇢ Taxes. Nobody likes paying taxes, but what are the costs of recent tax reductions? The Bush tax cuts, which reduced the top income tax rate and dividend income tax rate and eliminated the estate tax, clearly favored the very rich to the detriment of the rest. The 2001 cut alone, once fully phased in, would deliver 42% of the benefits to 1% of the income distribution, that is, families earning more than $330,000 per year. Those cuts endanger the future of Social Security, Medicare, Medicaid, and unemployment payments, benefits that are far more important to the poor than to the rich.[23] The permanent elimination of the estate tax, already passed by the U.S. House, would shift some $1.5 billion a week from the public treasury to the bank accounts of the heirs of the nation's twenty thousand biggest fortunes,[24] something that on June 8, 2006, the Senate declined to do—at least for the time being.[25] Tax cuts, along with increased defense spending, create treasury deficits that are being compensated for by reductions that diminish or endanger funding for Social Security, Medicare, Medicaid, unemployment compensation, food assistance, education, and other programs that are more important for the poor than for the rich.[26]

Tax cut proponents are divided, as Paul Krugman explains,[27] into two groups on the basis of tax doctrine, though both favor cuts for the rich. (1) Supply-side economics claims that the government can cut taxes without severe reduction in public spending. Tax reductions on dividend income of the rich generate investment incentives, and hence long-term growth. Krugman denies that this is a genuine economic theory; it rather arose as a political effort to convince the American people—falsely—that tax-cuts could be painless. (2) The "starve-the-beast" position advocates tax-cuts precisely in order to force severe reductions in public spending. The reduction in tax revenue shrinks the government and makes social benefit programs unaffordable. The intention is to move the country back to a time prior to the social benefits conferred by New Deal and Great Society legislation. Krugman points out that the power currently lies with the "starve-the-beast" faction.

It is a little puzzling that Americans are so up-in-arms about their taxes. Middle-income Americans have seen little change in their overall taxes in the last thirty years. The rate for the highest tax bracket, however (35%), is half what it was in the 1970s. The total tax take in 2002 was 26.3% of the U.S. Gross Domestic Product; comparable 1999 figures were 38.2% in Canada, 45.8% in France, and 52.2% in Sweden.[28]

As summarized by Nicholas Confessore,[29] the three primary goals of the Bush tax policy are to eliminate taxes on wealth and investment (interest, dividends, capital gains); to motivate the middle class to resist tax increases by taxing only wages, not investment income; and to create a revenue stream that reduces the government to the size it was before the Depression. Given the thrust of this agenda, the Christian Right's support for Bush is very troubling.[30] For example, in 2002, conservative Alabama governor Bob Riley decided that as a Christian he needed to make some very modest changes in the Alabama tax structure to readjust its preference for the rich, who paid income taxes at a rate of 3%, and its disadvantage to the poor, whose tax rates reached 12%. The plan was rejected by 68% of the voters in a state where 90% of the population say they are Christians. Another example: the Christian Coalition of America, founded in 1989 "to preserve, protect and defend the Judeo-Christian values that made this the greatest nation in history," proclaimed that its legislative priority would be "making permanent President Bush's 2001 federal tax cuts."

It appears that our country is not prepared to give up entitlements such as Social Security and Medicare, yet the Bush administration has refused to raise taxes. As Krugman suggests, this leaves borrowing as a short-term way to bridge the gap between tax revenue and spending, but sooner or later a choice must be made.[31] Will we choose to be a country in which only the rich can live decently, or one in which all are enabled to do so?

→ Social Security. For twenty years, Wall Street has been predicting an imminent shortfall of Social Security when the baby boomers retire, and has called for the privatization of Social Security. The transparent reason for the prophecy is the profit that the investment industry would rake in from servicing the accounts made possible by privatization.[32] The Bush administration then picked up the scare tactics and crisis-mongering of Wall Street, initiating a potentially self-fulfilling campaign: if enough people were to become convinced that Social Security is headed for bankruptcy, then it would lose public support, and Congress would be forced to enact privatization.[33]

This is how it would work: Younger workers would be allowed to divert a portion of their payroll taxes into private individual accounts and, upon retirement, supplement their diminished Social Security benefits with whatever had accumulated in those private accounts. Since, however, the diverted money would not be available to pay benefits to current retirees, the government would have to borrow to pay those benefits.[34] This privatization plan would set aside the original intention of Social Security, which was to provide security, not wealth. Privatization would, therefore, be a disaster because it would subject to market risks and uncertainties what is now a guaranteed annual income for life.[35] About half of Americans also have private pension plans—which are also in trouble—but for two-thirds of the elderly, Social Security provides the majority of day-to-day income. For the poorest 20%, about seven million people, Social Security is all they have. In 2000, 48% of them would have been below the poverty line without Social Security.[36] This is why the system must not be exposed to the risks of the market.

Admittedly, there are actuaries and economists inside and outside the Social Security agency who think that the system needs small adjustments to stay solvent, but they reject the crisis view and hold that modest measures like the following would enable the system to continue functioning as it has since 1935: (1) gradually raise the cap on income subject to the pay-roll tax, which would entail a small tax increase on people who make more than $90,000; (2) increase the payroll tax in fifty years; (3) make modest cuts in benefits; (4) gradually redeploy the trust fund into assets that Congress could not tap for any purpose.[37]

Although Bush, in the face of considerable opposition, admitted defeat in the fall of 2005, he did not give up on privatization. His 2007 fiscal year budget included the estimated impact from the creation of personal private accounts, and forces gathered to advance this program. The "impact" referred to in the budget document would be $712 billion diverted from the Social Security trust funds. This depletion of the trust funds in order to pay for private accounts would diminish the ability of Social Security to pay full guaranteed benefits and subject our children and grandchildren to deficits, higher taxes, and lower benefits.[38]

→ **Consumption and Debt.** Real wages have been declining in America for four decades—due in considerable part to the loss of manufacturing jobs—but there has been no parallel weakening of the American desire to consume. Into this gap between income and spending has stepped the lending industry, offering artificial purchasing power in the form of loans. Even in debt, we spend rather than save. In 1981, Americans saved a net 8.5% of national income, but by 2003 this had fallen to 1.2%. Because we have relinquished our manufacturing base, much of what we buy has to be imported from abroad. This then creates an enormous trade deficit that generates a correspondingly large national debt, owed especially to China.[39] To put some figures to this: Between 2000 and 2004, household debt increased by 39%. During this period, mortgage debt rose from $4.4 trillion to $7.5 trillion, and total household mortgage and consumer debt rose from $6.5 trillion to $10.2 trillion. In 2003 and 2004, the trade deficit in manufactured goods rose from $470 billion to $552 billion.[40]

The American consumers have to bear most of the responsibility for these developments, but the credit card industry and the government share complicity. The credit card companies lure consumers with interest rates of 1% and 2%, but once they are hooked, they may see increases to 6%, 11%, 20% or 30%. The government is complicit in interest policies and in the deregulation of the credit card industry, and also in a campaign of rhetoric in which debt and consumer spending are touted as a way to strike back at al-Qaeda by supporting our economy. As Kevin Phillips put it, never before have political leaders urged increased debt on an already debt-burdened nation to rally the economy.[41] A population deeply in debt is vulnerable to economic events that cannot be readily foreseen or controlled. Phillips has suggested that a 10% to 20% price slump in the housing market would be devastating;[42] indeed, it has been recently argued that the housing bubble is already bursting.[43]

Government Abuse, Distortion, and Neglect of Knowledge

In an increasingly complex world, we need all of the knowledge (and, hopefully, wisdom) that we can acquire to make good decisions and live productive and useful lives. To deprive a population of knowledge is an injustice; yet that is just what the U.S. government has been doing.

Hendrik Hertzberg has given a compact, yet comprehensive account of the posture of the Bush Administration:

> From the beginning, the Bush White House has treated science as a nuisance and scientists as an interest group—one that, because it lies outside the governing conservative coalition, need not be indulged. That's why the White House . . . has altered, suppressed, or overridden scientific findings on global warming; missile defense; H.I.V./AIDS; pollution from industrial farming and oil drilling; forest management and endangered species; environmental health, including lead and mercury poisoning in children and safety standards for drinking water; and non-abstinence methods of birth control and sexually-transmitted-disease prevention. . . . All this and more has been amply documented in reports from congressional Democrats and the Union of Concerned Scientists, in such leading scientific publications as *Nature, Scientific American, Science,* and *The Lancet.*[44]

→ **The Environment and Global Warming.** Tim Flannery's authoritative book *The Weather Makers* reports that we now have proof positive, from a study published in *Science*, of the global reality of the earth's warming. The earth now absorbs more energy than it radiates into space. The principal source of this warming is the increase of carbon dioxide (CO_2) in the atmosphere. CO_2 is a colorless, odorless gas that helps regulate atmospheric balance; it is also a waste product of burning fossil fuels that we create every time we drive a car, cook a meal, or turn on the light. We know precisely the size of our atmosphere and the volume of pollutants we are pouring into it.[45]

As Flannery points out, concern for the environment is not only a matter of caring for the earth as God's creation but is also a justice issue, bearing on whether some peoples will be able to live at all and on our own obligation to reduce inequality. Global warming threatens the Inuits of the North with the loss of their traditional foods, like seals, and also with the loss of their very land to the sea. Similarly, five Pacific and Indian Ocean atoll nations are threatened with destruction by the loss of coral reefs, rising seas, and intensifying weather events. Such developments fly in the face of the Universal Declaration of Human Rights, which states that "everyone has the right to a nationality" and that "no one shall be arbitrarily deprived of his property." They also violate the United Nations Covenant on Civil and Political Rights, which states that "in no case may a people be deprived of its own means of subsistence."[46]

Americans emit three times more CO_2 per person per year than do Europeans, and over 100 times more than the citizens of the least developed countries. Therefore, it seems especially blameworthy that ours is one of four nations—the other three being Australia, Monaco and Liechtenstein—that have not signed the Kyoto Protocol, an international treaty designed to reduce CO_2 emissions.

The road to Kyoto began in 1985, and the treaty received enough signatories to put it into effect in 2004.[47] For the "first target period" named in the treaty, 2008–2012, the European Union was to reduce its 1990 emissions by 8%, and the U.S., by 7%. The U.S. objected that no constraints were imposed on the developing nations for the 2008–2012 period and claimed that this gave the poor nations an unfair economic advantage. In 1997, the U.S. Senate passed a resolution declaring that it would reject any treaty that did not require reductions on the part of the developing nations. Others argued that it was fair to exempt the poor nations for the first period since it was the developed countries that had created the problem.[48] The U.S. and Australia rejected the treaty because they feared it would slow economic growth and thus be too costly, but neither country carried out any careful cost analyses, with the result that the debate has been informed by highly varied estimates from special interest groups. However, studies by highly qualified university economists have argued that the emission decreases required to reach the 2012 target would be modest and would not bankrupt our nations.[49]

Neither has the U.S. or Australia bothered to determine the cost of not complying with the Kyoto Protocol. Striking statistics reveal how foolish this failure is. The National Climatic Data Center lists seventeen weather events that occurred between 1998 and 2002 that cost over a billion dollars apiece, including droughts, floods, fire seasons, hail storms, heat waves, ice storms, and hurricanes. Since the 1970s, insurance losses have risen at an annual rate of around 10 percent, reaching $100 billion in 1999. Should they continue at this rate, such losses would threaten our entire economic system, for by about 2065 the cost of damage from climate change would equal the total value of everything the world produced in the course of a year.[50]

Early on, Bush set out to change the environmental regulations required by what was called "new-source review." While he had little success getting his agenda through Congress, by the use of under-the-radar regulatory changes, strategic political appointments, and bureaucratic directives he succeeded in replacing the E.P.A.'s tough clean-air programs with a more industry-friendly regimen. This regimen decimated the new-source review requirements regarding the installation of pollution-control devices when a plant made significant improvements. The American Lung Association and a coalition of environmental groups issued a report calling the rule changes "the most harmful and unlawful air-pollution initiative ever undertaken by the federal government."[51]

A recent article[52] reports that the President has now conceded that global climate change is serious and largely man made, and that he has agreed to discuss with others what should be done.

→ Intelligent Design. Fortunately, a federal judge has ruled that schools in a Pennsylvania school district may not mention intelligent design as an alternative to evolutionary theory. The judge stated that intelligent design is a religious view, a mere re-labeling of creationism, and not a scientific theory.[53] It is hard to say, however, how long it will take for this judgment to seep down into the minds of a significant majority of Americans. According to recent Gallup poll, 45% of us believe that the Book of Genesis gives us the true account of human origins; 64% of us (including secular humanists, liberal Democrats, and believers in evolution) were open to teaching *creationism* (not just intelligent design) in addition to evolution, and 38% favored replacing evolution with creationism. President Bush supports teaching both evolution and intelligent design so that people can understand what the debate is all about.[54]

The belief that both evolution and creationism, or intelligent design, can or should be taught in public school science classes obscures a true understanding of our world and shows that large numbers of presumably educated Americans do not really understand what a scientific theory is. Evolution and intelligent design are not two varieties of scientific theory. A scientific theory must rest on testable physical evidence. Intelligent design does not take the biblical account of origins literally, but it does maintain that the complexity of the world requires the postulation of a uniquely intelligent cosmic designer. But the reality of such a transcendent cosmic designer is not physically testable. Intelligent design is not a scientific theory.

Contrary to one of the arguments for intelligent design, reasoning from a watch to an intelligent watch designer and maker is *not* analogous to reasoning from the cosmos to a super-intelligent and transcendent designer. The former case reasons from a finite, physical, observable watch to a finite, physical, observable designer. Both belong broadly to the same category. The second case reasons from the finite, physical, observable cosmos to an infinite, spiritual, non-observable designer. These two do *not* belong to the same broad category. The reality of the transcendent designer cannot be tested. Again, though some version of intelligent design might be an adequate *theological* position, this is not a *scientific* theory.

→ **Abortion, Sex Education, and Birth Control.** The anti-abortion lobby has produced disastrous results, as Christian Right groups in America like American Life League and Focus on the Family have helped to drive Bush administration policy to cut funding for any international women's groups that counsel women abroad about even the possibility of having an abortion. The result has been more restrictive abortion laws that have helped to force some 20 million illegal procedures worldwide every year, causing more than 700,000 deaths annually, according to the World Health Organization.[55]

Abortions are relatively rare in countries where prospective mothers have knowledge about and access to contraception. Such knowledge has other benefits as well. Funding for sex education is increasing strongly in the U.S., but unfortunately there are usually prohibitions against any mention of contraceptives. Some 60% of American teenagers report having sex before the age of eighteen; so do their Canadian and European counterparts, but American girls, deprived of proper sex education, are five times as likely as French girls to have a baby, and seven times as likely to have an abortion, and seventy times as likely to have gonorrhea, as Dutch girls. Moreover, the incidence of H.I.V./AIDS among American teenagers is five times that of teenagers in Germany.[56]

The Cultivation of the Christian Right

I have already mentioned the Christian Right with regard to specific issues (and will again). This peculiar connection between religion and politics in America deserves more focused attention here. I accept Mark Taylor's identification of the Christian Right as constituted by a merging of conservative Protestant theology (though some Catholics are also involved) with a commitment to a conservative political agenda, most recently that of the Bush administration, characterized by nationalistic, if not imperialistic, domestic and foreign policies.[57] It is the merger that is particularly dangerous and troubling. From one side, the Bush political agenda has become an integral part of the Christian Right's agenda, and the government's political power entices Christian communities to emulate the government by attaining and exercising power on its own. From the other side, the unique energy and authority of religion becomes attached to the government's political project. The church has a theological and moral responsibility to be related to the state—but with a space between them. The church should pay attention to what the government is doing and be ready to speak and act upon a critical word. The interpenetration of the two is dangerous, however. Each can be distorted and weakened by the power of the other.

For example, Jim Wallis[58] reported a 2002 speech in which George Bush took words from the Gospel of John about the light shining in the darkness and the darkness not being able to overcome it (1:5), detached them from their contextual reference to the eternal Word of God, and attached them to America and its values. This kind of rhetoric uses the power of religious language to give our government's aggressive expansionism an aura of universal significance[59] and an undue power to rival God. Note that the Christian imagery does not disappear, but it is divested of its own meaning and references, and its power is transferred to the state.

Again, recall that I referred in Chapter 3 to a sermon by a New York minister who grieved at the loss of "America's Cathedrals" in the fall of the Twin Towers. Here secular commitment to free enterprise dominates genuine Christian faith, to the point that the latter disappears and the economic forces symbolized by the Twin Towers become the object of the church's faith.

Yet again: Michael Lerner[60] quotes a leader of the Christian Right who has proposed a blatant theocratic imperialism:

Christians have an objective, a commission, a holy responsibility to reclaim the land for Jesus Christ—to have dominion in civil structures, just as in every other aspect of life and godliness. But it is dominion we are after. Not

> just a voice. It is dominion we are after. Not
> just influence. It is dominion we are after. Not
> just equal time. It is dominion we are after.
> World conquest. That's what Christ has com-
> missioned us to accomplish. We must win the
> world with the power of the Gospel. And we
> must never settle for anything less. . . . Thus,
> Christian politics has as its primary intent the
> conquest of the land—of men, families, insti-
> tutions, bureaucracies, courts and governments
> for the Kingdom of Christ.

Here the merging of the religious and political
has transferred political power—or at least the will
to political power—from the political to the religious order so that now, some who claim to represent Christ seek to dominate everything politically.

One final example, an opinion column by Cal
Thomas, shows the reverse movement in which
religion comes to dominate and distort the social-
economic-political order.   Scripture is read in
such a way as to limit its applicability to justice
issues. Thomas urged that Christians should not
get involved in the politics of global warming and
the environment, since Jesus has told us what our
responsibilities are, and we have no cause or obli-
gations beyond these things: feeding the hungry,
clothing the naked, visiting prisoners, and praying
for enemies.[61] This way of reading Scripture restricts
it to its most literal and limited meanings, failing to
ask what implications might be drawn from Scripture taken as a whole and from its social context.

Such interpretation of Scripture thus constrains
the scope of social justice—or is it the other way

around, that a lack of commitment to comprehensive social justice has constrained the reading of Scripture? At a practical level, can we imagine a more flagrant and senseless failure to consider social context in applying Christian ethical norms? How will we feed the hungry, clothe the naked, or do the other things required to address the needs of the least advantaged if we abuse our planet to the point that there are no resources left with which to do them?

The Imperial Presidency

A recent article describes how over the last two hundred years the U.S. has been transformed from a traditional republic to a democratic nation run in large measure by a single executive. This is quite contrary to the Constitution, which intended for the legislative branch to be the most powerful. The Bush administration has augmented this tendency, and Congress has done virtually nothing to curb the expansion of presidential power. The Constitution lays down principles for the separation of powers, but which branch of government actually has the most power depends on which one asserts itself most boldly in give-and-take struggle. Currently the President and the Executive Branch have the upper hand.[62]

Bush himself, as reported by Bob Woodward, announced: "I'm the commander—see, I don't need to explain—I do not need to explain why I say things. That's the interesting thing about being president. Maybe somebody needs to explain to me why they say something, but I don't feel like I owe anybody an explanation."[63] And Bush has plenty of encouragement from his administration. According to John Yoo, a former Justice Department official who wrote the crucial memos justifying the government's torture policies, the imperial or unitary presidency is the idea that as commander-in-chief the president is the sole judge of the law. He is not bound by treaties, and has inherent authority to subordinate the whole government—including Congress and the courts—whenever he decides to do so. This is the cornerstone of the Bush doctrine of the presidency, and is maintained by Attorney General Gonzales and by the White House.[64]

On the basis of the President's authority as commander-in-chief of the military, administration lawyers have argued that Bush has the unilateral power to launch a pre-emptive invasion without Congressional approval; order indefinite detention of whomever he regards as an "enemy combatant"; authorize indiscriminate torture; prosecute non-American detainees in "military commissions" devised by his administration, and offering few protections; and spy on Americans without court warrants. In this regard, Justice Robert Jackson has written that holding that a president can escape the legal control of executive powers by assuming his military role is a sin against free government that is beyond expiation.[65]

Bush has made extensive use of "signing statements" to revise or ignore some 750 laws. A signing statement is a memorandum, issued along with legislation even as the president signs it, by which he reserves the right not to enforce the legislation if he thinks it violates the Constitution or national interests. According to the *New York Times*, two theories are at work here: that a president's intent in signing a bill trumps the intent of Congress in writing it, and that a president can claim power without restriction or supervision by the courts or Congress. These are the pet theories of Samuel Alito, whom Bush appointed to the Supreme Court.[66]

In sum, the Bush administration's policy to fight any restraint on the president's power has frayed the democratic fabric of a government based on Constitutional checks and balances. The invocation of the president's unitary power in order to enhance security has played upon American anxieties in such a way that civil and human liberties have been diminished.[67]

The Erosion of Civil Liberties

Free speech and the free press are under attack from various forms of domestic surveillance. The Pentagon is monitoring peaceful anti-war groups and protests using videotaping, Internet monitoring, the collection of names of those who criticize the government. There is a toll-free number by means of which one can report a fellow American to the military. Even Quaker meetings are under surveillance.[68] Quite ordinary citizens may be targeted, and the channels for doing so can be initially very unofficial. For example, a North Carolina high school teacher had her students do a project to illustrate freedoms provided by the Bill of Rights. One student illustrated the right to dissent by preparing a picture of Bush next to his own hand in a thumbs-down position. A Wal-Mart employee in the photo department reported this to police, who called the Secret Service, who decided to investigate the case. Both the teacher and the student were questioned for no other reason than to try to frighten people out of dissent.

There are many such stories.[69] Whistleblowers who expose government misconduct have long been valued and praised. In fact, government workers are required to report waste, fraud, abuse, and corruption to the appropriate authorities. But a Los Angeles County prosecutor who did just this was demoted and transferred, and the Supreme Court recently upheld his punishment. Apparently the primary "duty" now of government employees is not to protect the country by truthfully reporting violations, but to be blindly loyal to their supervisors.[70]

I mention briefly three other endangerments. First, our major media are owned by corporations for whom, as a matter of principle, profit is always the major consideration. Second, the renewed USA Patriot Act still gives the government access to such "tangible items" as records from libraries and bookstores. And third, the new Supreme Court, with the help of Bush appointees, Justices Roberts and Alito, has removed a protection against unlawful search: the police no longer need to knock and wait.[71]

The most dramatic news regarding civil liberties was the revelation in December 2005 that the National Security Agency, which is charged with monitoring international conversations (including those connecting within the U.S.), was spying on American citizens without a court warrant.[72] In 1978, the Foreign Intelligence Surveillance Act established the FISA Court, whose job was to determine whether to grant warrants to the NSA or FBI to monitor the communications of American citizens and legal residents. Historically this court has been very friendly to requests for warrants from the executive branch: in fact, the government is allowed to eavesdrop for three days before it even has to ask for a warrant. The Bush administration, however, was unwilling to show probable cause that any American they wanted to target was somehow connected to a terrorist group; therefore, Bush decided in the fall of 2001 that he would not be bound by the FISA Court. By bypassing the court, the president no longer meets the requirement to secure a warrant from the Court to put an American on the watch list; now the decision may be left to the vague and subjective "reasonable belief" of the NSA shift supervisor. As a result, while prior to 2001 perhaps a dozen Americans every year were named by the Court for surveillance, as many as 5,000 citizens have been targeted in the last four years.

The method of surveillance is not so primitive as "wiretapping." Instead, tens of millions of telephone calls, e-mails, faxes, instant messages, and Web searches are run through a complex system of supercomputers every hour. These communications are screened for particular names, telephone numbers, Internet addresses, and trigger words and phrases. Any communications containing flagged information are forwarded by the computer for further analysis. Formerly, but not since 2001, putting the name of an American on the watchlist at this point required a Court warrant.

The NSA is close to achieving its ultimate goal: intercepting and reviewing every word zapped into or out of or through the United States. Senator Frank Church, who led the first probe into the NSA, warned in 1975 that given the present technology, if our government were ever taken over by a dictator, the tyranny would be total. There would be no place to hide and no ability to plan resistance because all communication would be within government reach.

On August 17, 2006, a District Judge struck down Bush's warrantless surveillance program, saying that it violated the rights to free speech and privacy as well as the Constitutional separation of powers. The administration plans to appeal and to do everything it can to continue the program.[73]

8.

What Have We Been Doing since 9/11? Foreign Affairs

In this chapter I will touch on two issues: briefly, American unilateralism and, at greater length, the Iraqi war, the latter being a colossal instance of the former. I will also place that war in a theological context, provided by Isaiah and others, and in the larger historical context of American imperialism.

American Unilateralism

The U.S. violated the UN Charter in going to war with Iraq, and President Bush made the UN irrelevant by ignoring it when it did not go along with what he wanted. By refusing to submit the International Criminal Court treaty to the U.S. Senate for ratification, Bush chose to depreciate the effort of 92 nations to move beyond the justice of winners over losers and to give international criminal justice a more impartial and permanent basis. Bush's refusal to accept the Kyoto Protocol signals that the United States declines to assume its responsibility for protecting the world's air, earth, and seas, which are the common resource of all peoples.[1]

The Iraq War and American Imperialism

→ A Theological Perspective: The Impulse to Empire. What propelled the renewed and intensified impulse to American empire in certain quarters during the period 1990–2003? I will look later at political and economic motives for the invasion of Iraq, but here I consider the broader and deeper existential basis for the imperial impulse. One answer is that the imperial impulse resulted from the strong sense of power emanating from our victory in the Cold War and our emergence as the sole superpower. We were required in that moment to do something with the victory and to achieve our providential mission.[2] Another more complex answer, one I find finally more convincing, is that the impulse arose paradoxically from the fusion of this sense of power with a repressed sense of weakness and threat. The American resort to force is both an expression of our actual military power and a reaction to the decline in our economic power, which threatens to worsen.[3]

In *God and Human Suffering*, Douglas John Hall observes insightfully that when a society is unable to face the possibility of devastating future suffering, it represses the threat and the fear of it, producing a case of collective self-deception. In the case of the Iraq war, our conscious cover story is that our military power will be able to overcome all threats and obstacles; the unconscious real story, however, is that we face a genuine threat. This sense of menace, though (relatively) unconscious, cannot be completely eradicated. But rather than look at what we may be doing to cause it—the gap between rich and poor, the excessive debt, the environmental degradation, and the imperialism that earns the world's hatred—we select an external enemy on which to fix blame. As Hall puts it, an empire always needs an enemy to avoid facing the flaws in its own triumphant self-image.[4] All of that being true, however, does not nullify the complicating fact that terrorism is a reality that must be resolutely faced.

→ **From Disposition to Action.** The Bush government's march into war with Iraq can also be grasped theologically by placing it in a configuration suggested by Isaiah (recall Chapter 3). Arrogance (Isa. 1:2; 2:8, 11-12) and blindness or ignorance (Isa. 1:3; 5:13, 20-21) penetrate and interact upon each other reciprocally. Ignorance, a misunderstanding of the order of the universe (Isa. 5:20; 29:15-16), causes people to attribute excessive value to themselves (arrogance). But this causes people to have a distorted view of reality (blindness or ignorance). Arrogance produces blindness and ignorance, which produces greater arrogance, which produces greater blindness and ignorance, and so it continues. This vicious circle generates unjust, harmful actions (Isa. 1:4, 16-17; 5:7-9; 19:11-15): imperialism, war, and their attendant evils.

In the case of our country, the arrogance is seen in our belief that we have all of the answers and can pursue our own interests in total disregard for the UN Charter, world opinion, and the ruinous consequences for other people. Nowhere is this more blatantly expressed than in the writing of political columnist Charles Krauthammer, in whose eyes the best policy for the United States will be to exercise the strength and will to lead a unipolar world, unashamedly laying down the rules of world order and being prepared to enforce them.[5]

Our arrogance produces blindness and ignorance. Specifically, the Bush government was blind to intelligence reports that Iraq did not have WMDs because it already believed, and wanted to believe, the opposite. It was blind to the need to plan for the postwar period; blind to the fact we would not be welcome as liberators; blind to the power of insurgency and unaware of how to fight a counter-insurgent war; and blind to the fact that Islam and the nature of Iraqi society would pose obstacles to the establishment of Western-style democracy.[6] The cost of fighting the insurgency led to the abandonment of efforts to reconstruct the Iraqi water and sanitation systems.[7]

Moreover, the U.S. government blindly believed that the Kurds, Shiites and Sunnis all wanted to build a unified state,[8] and that France and other dissenting nations on the Security Council would return to the fold once they witnessed our welcome in Baghdad.[9] Furthermore, according to Kevin Phillips, the Bush administration believed that our victory would flood the world with oil and break the back of OPEC. Sabotage and the relentless insurgency ironically produced the opposite.[10]

→ A Very Brief Historical Sketch of American Imperialism. *Imperialism* can be understood as the policy and practice of one nation's extending its power, authority, or influence over another nation(s). Some hold that imperialism in the proper sense entails direct territorial acquisition; others hold that it can include indirect control over the political or economic life of another area.[11] I accept the second definition. Some advocates have claimed that the American empire is qualitatively different from its earlier European precursors in that the American ambition is not just to make the U.S. the dominant world power but to make all other states reflect the American version of capitalism.[12] Because I propose to understand the invasion of Iraq as yet another chapter in a longer history of American imperialism, I offer a brief review of how that history was set in motion.

There is general agreement that American imperialism, properly speaking, began with the Spanish-American War, when our nation abandoned the advice of Washington and Jefferson to stay out of foreign entanglements. This military activation of our imperialistic impulse was motivated by a need, felt in diverse circles—politicians, military experts, business leaders, economists, and other intellectuals—to acquire colonies in order to bolster U.S. military power and to provide markets for American capital. Another imperialistic impulse, harking back to the late 1880s, was the desire to fulfill a historic religious mission, a "manifest destiny," to civilize and Christianize the world, a vision to which President McKinley was won over in 1898.[13] These imperialist impulses received an added push from various groups in the U.S. who agitated for military intervention in Cuba against Spain's repression of a Cuban independence movement. After McKinley sent the battleship Maine to Havana, it blew up on February 15, 1898, killing 266 Americans. Though likely an accident, the explosion became a pretext for war against Spain, declared in April of 1898. The American victory came quickly, in July of that year, and engendered a national euphoria, the beginning of our "illusions of omnipotence."[14]

After the Spanish surrender, the American military took possession of the former Spanish colonies—Puerto Rico, Guam, and the Philippines—and McKinley resisted the attempts of his critics in Congress to grant independence to these possessions. He installed a military government to rule Cuba and a colonial administrator in the Philippines. The U.S. military then fought a fourteen-year war against a Filipino insurgency, deploying 120,000 troops, of whom 4,000 died. Some 200,000 Filipinos also were killed—soldiers and civilians alike—and American troops committed atrocities.[15]

During these same years, Theodore Roosevelt began a career that would make him the foremost symbol of an aggressive American imperialism. He joined the McKinley administration in 1897, and soon after wrote to a friend that he hoped for a general national buccaneering expedition that would drive the Spaniards out of Cuba and the English out of Canada. Roosevelt championed the idol of the warrior male and was committed to a "muscular" version of Christianity. He prodded McKinley into annexing the Philippines and setting up a military government in Cuba, then backed the suppression of the Filipino rebels and led the coverup and whitewash of atrocities committed by American troops. Roosevelt was capable of learning from his mistakes, however. He later lost some of his enthusiasm for the imperialistic project and came to regard the annexation of the Philippines as a mistake. He never fully abandoned imperialism, however, and continued to believe it to be an unqualified blessing for the people it colonized.[16]

Early on, Woodrow Wilson as well believed that American imperialism was contributing to a more peaceful, prosperous and moral civilization; but after the outbreak of World War I he came to see that it was the very struggle for colonies among imperial powers that precipitated war. Until April 1917, Wilson worked for a peace without victory, attempting to reconcile the opposing sides in that war, believing that a triumph by either one would destabilize peace and lead to future wars. He nevertheless took the U.S. to war on the side of the Allies because of renewed German submarine warfare against American shipping. At the war's end he urged a magnanimous settlement with Germany, but the other Allies rejected that.[17]

Wilson believed that lasting peace could be achieved only by dismantling the imperialistic system and replacing it with a new League of Nations and a new world order that would discourage the scramble for colonies. Wilson maintained that America should be the senior partner in the League, leading the world to liberty and establishing the kingdom of God on earth; but he believed this could not be achieved by imposing freedom and democracy on the unwilling or by working unilaterally. The U.S. should rather work in concert with other nations to establish a global democracy composed of independently self-determining states that would provide collective security for each other.

The U.S. Senate rejected the League of Nations treaty.[18]

With Roosevelt's aggressive expansionism on the one hand, and on the other, Wilson's rejection of imperialistic colony-building and his idealistic goal of America's leading the world by multilateral cooperation to establish a world democracy with collective security, the key elements had been enunciated that would, in varying combinations, form American foreign policy across the decades and into the Iraq war.

→ **The War for Oil.** There is another, long-term war within which we need to contextualize 9/11 and the Iraq war. Andrew Bacevich points out that the conventional way of structuring war history from 1914 to the present is: (1) World War I (1914–1918); (2) World War II (1939–1945); (3) the Cold War (World War III) (1947–1989); (4) an interlude of relative peace (1990s); and (5) the war on terror (World War IV) (9/11/01–). Bacevich believes, however, that a different narrative is more realistic. He argues that "World War IV" actually began in 1980 and so overlies a part of the Cold War. The two conflicts are distinct, however, because the American-Soviet conflict is not the defining factor in World War IV; oil is, and so I will refer to Bacevich's "World War IV" as "the Oil War." This scheme allows us to recognize the Iraq war, and its connection to 9/11, not as the beginning of World War IV, but as another chapter in a war begun years earlier.[19]

According to Bacevich, the Oil War began, ironically enough, with Jimmy Carter's 1980 State of the Union Address, in which he announced that any attempt by an outside force to gain control of the Persian Gulf region would be regarded as an assault on American vital interests and would be repelled by any means necessary. His intention was to assure the unimpeded flow of oil. Every American president since Carter has reaffirmed the Carter doctrine.[20] Of course, the policy behind this "war" can be traced back even further, to the pivotal 1945 agreement between Franklin Delano Roosevelt and King Saud of Arabia exchanging protection for oil,[21] and even further back to 1897, when a nervous Kuwaiti sheikh asked the British to assume a protectorate over Kuwait.[22]

→ **The Motives for the Iraq War.** The Iraq war belongs in the history I have just described. Prior to 9/11, Bush's position on foreign policy seems to have been a combination of nationalism and provincialism, but after the events of that day, disengagement and withdrawal gave way to an active project to "eradicate evil." Already on the twelfth day of the Bush administration, Donald Rumsfeld had invited his colleagues on the National Security Council to imagine a Middle East without Saddam Hussein, and 9/11 seems to have offered the opportunity for Bush's tough-guy, frontier mode to emerge. Less than two months after the U.S. invaded Afghanistan, Bush secretly ordered a war plan to smash the Iraqi government, and in March of 2003 we invaded Iraq without UN sanction.[23]

The Bush administration offered two motives for getting rid of Saddam Hussein: he possessed huge stock piles of WMDs, and he had a connection with al-Qaeda and bore responsibility for 9/11. Both of these claims have been shown to be fraudulent,[24] despite Secretary of Defense Rumsfeld's requests, on ten separate occasions, to the CIA to prove that Saddam and al-Qaeda were linked. Intelligence agents told reporters that they were pressured to make claims not supported by evidence.[25] Even if the Bush administration believed these charges against Saddam, they were still merely pretexts for a war that was proposed prior to 9/11 in order to advance the goal of world domination. The falsity of these two charges has nevertheless been no deterrent to Bush's continuing use of them to defend the Iraqi war. A Senate report, released on September 8, 2006, discloses a CIA assessment made in October 2005 that reiterates that prior to the Iraq war, Saddam did not have a relationship with the al-Qaeda operative Abu Musab al-Zarqawi. Nor is there evidence (contrary to a 2002 intelligence report) that Iraq was reconstituting its nuclear program or possessed biological weapons. Nevertheless, in a news conference on August 21, 2006, Bush said that we should imagine a world in which Saddam had the capacity to make WMDs, and that Saddam did have relations with al-Zarqawi.[26]

One additional motive for the war has been the oft-repeated claim that our intention is to spread democracy and freedom to Iraq and the whole Middle East. One will have to assess the extent to which this motive is an attempt to compensate for the falsity of the others and to conceal the real motives.[27] I refer to the widespread agreement that the twin motives behind the invasion of Iraq are tightly intertwined political and economic motives. Politically: to consolidate American power in the Middle East and change the political culture of the region. (Since Saudi Arabia could no longer be counted on as a secure base for American influence, the consolidation of American power would require not just control of Iraq, but its occupation and a change in its political and economic systems to conform to American purposes.[28]) Economically: to insure an unimpeded flow of oil. As Kevin Phillips has put it, this economic motive embraces several others: folding the oil objective into the war on terror; confirming the U.S. dollar's hegemonic role in oil sales; and convincing the Christian right that the destruction of the new Babylon (Baghdad) was a step on the way to Armageddon.[29] Given our hundred-year quest for Middle Eastern oil and our current pressing demand for it, it would be strange indeed if oil were *not* the major purpose of the war. Circumstantial evidence in support of this contention is that after the fall of Baghdad, looters were allowed to ravage almost everything; but the Oil Ministry, where the oil maps were located, was protected from harm.[30]

Where are we now, after four years of war in Iraq and with no idea about how to terminate it? Tens of thousands of people have been killed, and the Iraqi infrastructure has been wrecked. Al-Qaeda lives on, whether as a centralized organization or as a group of spin-offs (note the London airliner conspiracy). Open-ended occupation generates suicide bombers and new recruits to terrorism.[31] Sectarian violence and unrelenting insurgency make the elected government virtually non-functional. On September 18, 2006, UN Secretary-General Kofi Annan called on the Iraqi government to do more to build national unity lest the country collapse in the midst of full-scale civil war.[32]

The Political Aspect of Current American Imperialism

The Bush government's imperial agenda received political support from several different positions and movements.

→ **The Neoconservatives.** This movement came to exert the strongest influence on policy in the Bush administration. In the last months of the Cold War, a group of neoconservative policy makers and intellectuals began to argue that the time had come to create an America-dominated world order, a "Pax Americana," in which the American military would reach into every area of the world. The neocons resonated to the expansive nationalism of Theodore Roosevelt, but also favored Woodrow Wilson's ideal of spreading democracy worldwide, though they rejected Wilson's advocacy of multilateral international cooperation and disarmament. In sum, they stood for democratic globalism and unipolar dominion (the sole power being the U.S.). In the 1980s there had been "realist" neocons, but the idealist thrust came to define neoconservatism.[33]

The neoconservative project was laid out early in an important document, the *Defense Planning Guidance* prepared by Paul Wolfowitz under the direction of Defense Secretary Dick Cheney in early 1992. Its agenda was to replace "collective internationalism" with "benevolent domination by one power" as the leitmotif of American foreign policy. No nation or group of nations was to be able to challenge American global domination. The document was criticized for its chauvinism, but Cheney liked it, and in January 1993 signed on to a revised version of it.[34]

In 1997 William Kristol and Robert Kagan, along with help from others, founded an unipolarist foreign policy think tank called the Project for the New American Century, which basically reflected the politics and strategy of the Wolfowitz document. In January 1998, the PNAC wrote Bill Clinton a formal letter asking him to overthrow Saddam Hussein. In September 2000, the PNAC issued a position paper, *Rebuilding America's Defenses: Strategy, Forces, and Resources for a New Century,* in which it spelled out a strategy for global empire. Among other things it called for a great increase in defense spending and the size of the military, and proposed permanent new forces in southern Europe, Southeast Asia, and the Middle East. The PNAC had already advocated that we should strengthen our dominance in NATO and prevent any independent European security regime. In a June 2002 speech at West Point, Bush reserved the right to wage preemptive war in order to promote American principles throughout the world, and pledged to continue unipolar predominance.[35]

The goal of American foreign policy, according to the PNAC, should be to use American preeminence to maintain an international order friendly to American security, prosperity, and principles. The removal of Saddam Hussein and a permanent U.S. presence in the Persian Gulf were explicit parts of their strategy. Thus it turns out that 9/11 was not the cause of the Iraqi war but was simply the fortuitous occasion to begin a war that was already on the agenda.

→ **The Realists.** The "realists" in the Bush administration—Cheney, Rumsfeld, Rice, and others—agree with the neocons on the project of unipolar imperialism, but do not share their ardor for spreading democracy and "freedom" to other nations as a guiding principle. In contrast, they hold that the primary concern of U.S. policy should be to identify our vital interests, limit our efforts to promoting them, and pay minimal attention to anything else, including the building of world democracy. On this view, we have no special moral mission to the world.[36]

→ Pro-War Liberals. Perhaps the best representative of this position is Michael Ignatieff. In an article in *The New York Times Magazine*, he stated that our real reason for being in Iraq was to consolidate our position in the Arab world, but that this had been explained neither to the American people nor to the world. Moreover, the invasion was one more instance of our historical habit of unilateralism and intervention in the affairs of other nations.[37] In a succeeding series of articles,[38] however Ignatieff seems to take the position that if we do not assume the responsibility to spread democracy, no other nation can or will; our critics at home and abroad are wrong and unfair to doubt our idealism and to accuse us of doing the very things that Ignatieff himself said we were doing in the first article. Ignatieff's two positions seem quite contradictory to me, and I do not know how he would explain or resolve them.

There seems not to be a whole lot of difference between "pro-war liberals" like Ignatieff and the neocons regarding the Iraq war, with one important exception: Ignatieff believes that the U.S. should exercise its hegemony multilaterally, not unilaterally.[39]

→ **The Christian Right.** Bush has claimed divine approval for the invasion of Iraq: We have been called to help spread the freedom that is God's own gift to the whole world.[40] The Christian right has had its own theological reasons for believing him.

Over the past few decades, conservative Christians had been traumatized by the moral upheaval of the 1960s and by the Vietnam debacle. One eventual result was a regained respect for the military in the aftermath of Vietnam. Evangelicals came to see the armed forces as a place of virtue and a refuge for the sacred remnant of patriotic Americans. Military strength should be maintained, they believed, for military weakness was perceived as moral affliction. The anxiety resulting from the 1960s and Vietnam also prompted an appetite for the use of armed force on behalf of recovering a lost righteousness (for example, in opposition to Communism).[41] Such factors prepared the way for the Christian Right's response to 9/11 and the Iraq war. The Evangelical tendency to see moral issues in terms of sharp blacks and whites connected naturally with Bush's habitual and equally dualistic references to a war against evil.[42] Furthermore, the premillennial apocalyptic views of many Evangelicals have led them to support U.S. Middle East policy, especially our defense of Israel. Many in the Christian Right believe that we are already living in the end times, a conviction encouraged by the establishment of Israel, which they interpret as satisfying the biblical prophecy of the Jews' return to the Holy Land, a necessary precursor for the sequence of events culminating in the last days. According to this sequence, there will be a great tribulation giving rise to the appearance of the Antichrist, but also to his destruction in the battle of Armageddon; then comes the return of Christ and the inauguration of a thousand years of peace and justice.[43]

As Bacevich insightfully puts it, the Christian Right's support for a new American militarism in the wake of Vietnam presents a biting irony. While the more secular nations of Europe have become very wary of war in general, and critical of the Iraq war in particular, the most strongly Christian nation in the developed world has been quite ready to confer moral legitimacy on that war, or on almost any other American resort to force.[44]

→ Intimations of Moderation? The Bush administration's *National Security Strategy* (2006) seems to maintain the imperialistic position of the first Bush term; but Philip Gordon has recently argued in a circumspect article that, while the ideas and rhetoric have not changed, there has been a change in practice, tone, and style.[45] For example, Secretary of State Condoleezza Rice has effected a broad shift over the last year that displays a greater dimension of multilateralism, cooperation, and common sense; and President Bush, on a recent trip to Europe, tried to be more conciliatory.[46] Why is it, then, that Bush was confronted by angry crowds in Europe, and that a recent *Financial Times* poll showed that across the continent the U.S. was considered a greater threat to world peace than Iran or North Korea?[47]

There would appear to be several reasons. First, we should bear in mind that the supposed change in administration tone is new, and as yet unassimilated. Further, it can be of only limited effect, because it has been opposed by the Cheney/Rumsfeld contingent in the administration and undermined by the offensive behavior of John Bolton at the UN. Perhaps most importantly, it is not believed, and this skepticism results from the reasons that produced the change. That is, the administration changed tone because of the failure of the older approach. Bush has the nation bogged down in an unsuccessful war; the military is overstretched; our debt situation is horrific; and we have lost the respect and approval of the world. Thus other nations perceive the administration as changing for prudential and self-serving reasons, and not because there really is a new position. Fareed Zakaria surmises that for the administration to be taken seriously it would have to have an actually new and different policy, and would have to convince the world that it issues from a change of heart, not a change of circumstance.[48]

Finally, a perceived change in tone is not necessarily lasting. Philip Gordon conjectures[49] that a complete reversion to the foreign policy of the first Bush term could be triggered by another major terrorist attack on the U.S., by a provocative act by Iran, or by a dramatic turn in Iraq that would seem to suggest that the Bush project is working. Gordon believes it probable that pragmatism will continue, but who knows what might come from a president with a mission who is willing to accept massive risks?

Military Aspects of American Imperialism

→ **Military Doctrine and Spending.** Andrew Bacevich deplores the change in American military doctrine since Vietnam, which he describes as a change from seeing the military's task as defending the West from the threat of communist aggression and preserving freedom to a position that he calls "military metaphysics," meaning the tendency to see all international problems as military problems and to discount the likelihood of non-military solutions. The marriage of this frame of mind to the utopian goal of spreading democracy is the distinguishing element of contemporary American foreign policy, Bacevich argues, entailing the change from a defensive stance to one of preventive war, conquest, regime change, and imperialistic control.[50]

The new militarism manifests itself in the scope, cost and configuration of the American military. Our present day defense budge is 12% larger, adjusted for inflation, than the average Cold War budgets.[51] In 2002, U.S. defense spending was about $1 billion more than the combined spending of the world's next twelve biggest spenders (including Britain, France, Germany, Japan, China and Russia).[52] American spending accounts for 40% to 45% of all the defense spending of the world's 189 states.[53] The new militarism's increased propensity to use force leads to the normalization of war. Furthermore, a new "aesthetic of war" based on advanced technology makes war a kind of spectacle or spectator sport, in which the object is not so much to kill as to persuade by massive shows of force–a spectacle that American TV audiences can enjoy from a distance.[54] Another aspect of the new militarism, however, is that America has the power to carry out a persuasive threat of force; thus, Bush asserted that the U.S. would strike first, preventively, if need be. The aim of preventive war is not to warn or wound, but to kill quickly and efficiently with a first-round knockout.[55]

→ **Military Action.** Two other areas of military action bear mention here. Our insatiable appetite for oil has drawn the U.S. military increasingly to penetrate new areas. One such target is the Caspian Sea basin, which has huge reserves of oil and natural gas that are not under OPEC control. In order to gain access to these resources, and to counter Russian influence in the area and the competitive aspirations of European and Asian nations, the U.S. military was able during the Afghan war to establish thirteen new military bases in bordering ex-Soviet states. The U.S. now has more than half a million soldiers, spies, technicians, and other staff in these Eurasian countries. China has now also made access to the Caspian basin resources a cornerstone of its economic policies.[56]

Robert Kaplan has described in some detail the U.S. response to China's program of establishing widespread business and diplomatic outposts. China intends to protect its coasts and to extend its sphere of influence far into the Pacific and beyond. Kaplan argues that the U.S. needs to deter China without provoking it needlessly, something it can achieve through the U.S. Pacific Command, whose domain stretches from East Africa and includes the entire Pacific Rim. The strategy will make use of a complex configuration of security agreements and bases and a huge store of military aircraft and weaponry.[57] The optimal goal of such an approach would be to draw China into a Pacific Command alliance without a major war, but (Kaplan argues) we should be prepared for the latter. He takes it as a matter of course that our navy should patrol the Chinese mainland and have offensive naval craft that could land on Chinese beaches. He seems to assume that we have a right to tolerate no equal and to dominate the Far East.[58]

→ **The Abuse of Prisoners.** This is surely one of the most shameful concomitants of the expansion of militarism in the service of imperialism. In a practice called "rendition," suspected terrorists are seized and whisked away to foreign countries for harsh questioning—or torture. It is not known exactly how many people have been "rendered," but an NYU Law School report in 2003 estimated as many as 150. The most common destinations for rendered suspects are countries where torture has been practiced: Egypt, Morocco, Syria, and Jordan. Many of the suspects have never been charged with a crime, and they often vanish from their new homes.[59] European lawmakers reported that the CIA has conducted more than one thousand clandestine flights in Europe since 2001, some of them secretly taking away terror suspects to countries where they could face torture.[60] Both George Bush and Condoleezza Rice have denied that the U.S. practices rendition; Rice has refused to say whether the CIA has secret prisons in Europe.[61]

I turn to the issue of torture, including the torture of victims taken prisoner in battle or through "rendition" or in some other way. President Bush has stated that torture is never acceptable,[62] but whether torture has occurred evidently depends on how it is defined. Soon after 9/11, several figures in the Bush administration began advising him that the U.S. did not need to abide by the Geneva Conventions regarding prisoners in handling detainees from the war on terror, and Bush himself accepted this opinion. He also stated that we would seek to be humane in handling detainees, but that "military necessity" could override considerations of humaneness. State Department legal adviser William Taft advised the administration that its interpretation of the relevant documents was flawed, and another State Department lawyer maintained that the Geneva Conventions do not allow that any person is not covered by their standards. The State Department lost this argument, however, and reported that Bush decided to suspend the Geneva Conventions on January 8, 2002.[63] Meanwhile, an Assistant Attorney General, Jay S. Bybee, argued that for an act to be regarded as torture it must inflict pain so intense as to be difficult to endure, or else result in "organ failure." By this standard, acts that could be legally committed and should not be regarded as torture would include cruel, inhuman, and degrading treatment; threatening to kill a person; beating a person, or kicking a person in the stomach. In 2004, the Justice Department reversed this 2002 opinion,[64] but the fact remains that while many nations have practiced torture, the U.S. is the first to justify it openly.[65] Susan Sontag has argued that the abuse, along with the photographing of it, reflects the violence in the collective American psyche and the Bush administration's demonization of the enemy.[66] Lest this be dismissed immediately as an unjustified, America-hating indictment, a recent ABC/Washington Post poll found that 46% of Americans could agree to the physical abuse of others sometimes, and 35%, to outright torture in some cases.[67]

How far up the chain of command does the sanctioning of torture go? The administration has tended to push the responsibility down as far as possible to a few out-of-control enlisted men and women, but that position has been questioned from many sides. Could a few young people from average American towns have had the kind of knowledge of Islam, and especially its strictures regarding sex, to have dreamed up the techniques of religious humiliation and sexual degradation that were employed, including forced simulated sexual acts, the shaving off of beards, being leered at by women soldiers who rubbed their breasts against detainees, or smeared them with fake menstrual blood; or grabbing or kicking the genitals of detainees?[68] A panel commissioned to trace responsibility for offenses at Abu Ghraib concluded that there were failures of leadership all the way up to the Pentagon and Rumsfeld's office, failures that set the conditions that allowed for the abusive practices.[69] There is reason to believe that the resultant atrocities were committed in all of our prisons and by all branches of the service.[70]

The best answer to the question "How far up the chain of command?" is evident in the behavior of our vice president and president. In 2005, the administration was forced to accept legislation proposed by Senator John McCain to ban "cruel, inhuman, or degrading treatment" of prisoners held by the U.S. anywhere in the world. Vice President Cheney had led a White House lobbying effort to block this legislation, however, and after it was passed, attempted to exempt the CIA from its provisions (an exemption McCain rejected).[71] On June 29, 2006, the Supreme Court declared that detainees are in fact covered by Geneva Common Article 3 that prohibits cruel and inhumane treatment and grants human and legal protections. This decision nullified the military commissions that the administration had set up. The White House initially said that it would comply with the Court's ruling, but a day later its lawyers appeared on Capitol Hill to press Congress to approve military commissions similar to the ones the Court had said the President could not set up on his own. The administration apparently wants our forces to be able to violate the Geneva conventions without being chargeable for war crimes.[72]

Bush got his way. On September 27 and 28, 2006, both Houses of Congress approved a bill that established military commissions to prosecute terrorism suspects. The bill includes a blanket waiver for crimes Americans may have committed in the war on terror, and gives a president the power to jail pretty much anyone he wants to for as long as he wants, without charging them, and to reinterpret the Geneva Conventions unilaterally, deciding on his own what abusive interrogation methods are permissible. The definition of torture in the bill comes close to the very narrow one promulgated by the Justice Department in 2002 but reversed in 2004. It authorizes acts most normal people would regard as torture.[73] These events give us a pretty clear picture of how far up the chain of command the sanction of torture goes.

As an example of legal abuses at the Guantanamo prison that presumably will continue, the Naval Criminal Investigative Service has confiscated more than 1,100 pounds of letters and other personal documents belonging to Guantanamo detainees, documents that could have strengthened their defense. As a result, the detainees are limited in their ability to defend themselves, and attorney-client confidentiality has been compromised.[74] In 2004, Scott L. Silliman, Professor of Law and Executive Director of Duke University's Center on Law, Ethics, and National Security, offered a concise assessment of the moral and legal import of this reprehensible chapter in our national story. According to Silliman, there has been an apparent shift in our fundamental national principles from claiming to be a nation under the rule of law to being a nation that strives to find ways to avoid it.[75] As accurate as this statement is, it does not really do justice to the horrific evil wreaked upon the world by George W. Bush and his administration.

Economic Aspects of American Imperialism

We have already observed that the economic drive—gaining resources, acquiring opportunities for investment and markets for trade—motivated the imperial venture from the beginning. The economic realm also provides a means for controlling other nations. The agencies for effecting contemporary international economics were set up in July 1944, when 43 nations met in Bretton Woods, New Hampshire, and agreed to establish the International Monetary Fund and the World Bank. The purpose of these institutions was to stabilize monetary and credit systems, to assure the restoration of world trade, and to supply the huge volume of capital that would be needed for reconstruction, relief, and recovery. These agencies have had both successes and failures in reaching those goals.[76]

Kathryn Tanner[77] observes that the economy dominates our world today as never before because economic goods—money—are the basis for other important goods like education, health care, respect, and political power. Therefore, economic ruin threatens to bring down our whole way of life for both individuals and societies. Vassilis Fouscas and Bülent Gokay observe that our government's attempt to prevent such disaster by building up a world system of control makes us as dependent on instruments of economic control as we are on our military and our intelligence network.[78] The U.S. is not only a major actor in economic globalization, but practices economic imperialism through the instruments of globalization. I limit my remarks here to the dominant "neoliberal" model of globalization that is currently supported by big business and agencies, such as the World Trade Organization, that it has established.[79]

The American business establishment has supported globalization because European and Asian industry were challenging our economic hegemony and profit rates; to compete, American business needed access to cheaper labor and to new markets as developed-world markets reach the limits of their expandability. Further, capital available for investment has increased.[80] Big business has consequently advocated an integrated global economy that revolves around export-oriented trade, free of regulations and other trade barriers and characterized by a highly competitive private sector (no government corporations). Business regards the expected results as unequivocally beneficial: corporations will spread wealth, work, and technology around the world, with expanded options and cheaper prices for consumers. These benefits will accrue, not just to the developed nations, but to the former colonies that compose the undeveloped world as well.[81]

We should take a critical look at these expectations—and at the globalizing economic imperialism behind them.

→ **Ideology.** I have already discussed the ideology of free-market capitalism in Chapter 7; here I simply note the necessary features of international globalization. The arena of freedom in which the "free market" operates must be extended beyond national boundaries to include all nations. An "open economy" entails the free movement of goods, services, and investment funds across national borders, unfettered by government regulations. High tariffs, import quotas, and controls on foreign exchange must be removed since they impede growth. The government regulations that neo-liberal, free-trade ideology opposes are those intended to restrain raw corporate power, protect humane working conditions, and prevent environmental degradation.[82]

→ **Execution.** Advocates of neo-liberalism assume that the best hope for former colonies would be to adopt the neo-liberal program, as carried out by multinational and transnational corporations. Multinational corporations tend to take on the identities of the various countries in which they have operations, while transnational corporations generally seek to eliminate any national considerations as they try to maximize economies. One strategy of transnational corporations is to decentralize organization, through downsizing and outsourcing. In downsizing, "core" jobs (finance, marketing, proprietary technology) are divided from "contingent" jobs (labor), with the staff of the core jobs being reduced to a bare minimum and consolidated at corporate headquarters, while contingent jobs are outsourced to the lowest bidder, often a low-wage country in the undeveloped world.[83]

The global trend is corporations moving toward transnationalism, which has meant that they have come to see themselves, not so much as partners of states, but rather as independent entities transcending the boundaries of nations. Their wealth, often surpassing that of small nations, has enabled them to amass political power and to position themselves as the dominant political, economic, and social force of the twenty-first century.[84] The power that individual corporations may have is augmented by the fact that corporations can use the World Bank and the IMF to exercise economic control, especially over nations and peoples of the global South. The officials of these organizations have often had power to rewrite a nation's laws on such things as as trade policy, civil service requirements, labor, health care, and environmental and energy policy.[85] The current president of the World Bank is Paul Wolfowitz, one of America's most fervent neo-conservative imperialists. The more recent World Trade Organization is designed to serve as a global governing body for transnational corporate interests. Its mandate is to eliminate all barriers to international investment and competition. As an unelected global parliament, it has power to override economic and social policy decisions of democratic states. Such American corporations as IBM, AT&T, Time Warner, and Bank of America exercise power through their connections with American trade representatives in the WTO.[86]

One of the primary functions of the IMF and World Bank—as well as of commercial banks—has been to make loans to developing countries. Massive amounts of money on loan flowed into these countries in the 1970s, and when in the 1980s many of them could no longer pay the interest, the IMF and World Bank came to the rescue with a new class of loans—structural adjustment loans—that enabled these countries to continue paying interest but did not get them out of debt. The structural adjustments that the debtor nations had to accept in order to get the new loans required dismantling their own economic and social structure in favor of free-market and free-trade ideology, for example, by converting self-sufficient, small-scale agriculture to single-product export activities; reducing social and health services; eliminating price controls and imposing wage controls; and privatizing state enterprises.[87] Many of the debtor countries felt they had little choice but to sign on to the new loans. These loans, along with direct investment in the developing nations, have nurtured and augmented a small elite in the debtor nations, but all that has "trickled down" to populations who have only their labor to sell is a longer work week and reduced real wages. This left nations even deeper in debt, feeling like de facto colonies of the creditor nations. They are now left with results of decisions required by the loans: silted up dams, useless, crumbling roads to nowhere, empty high-rise office buildings, and ravaged forests and fields.[88]

Numerous factors reduced the capacity of these countries to service their debt: currency devaluations, mismanagement, and corruption, for example. But surely the most cynical cause of their failure has been exposed in dramatic detail by John Perkins in his *Confessions of an Economic Hit Man*. The phalanx of operatives known as Economic Hit Men (EHMs) is one of the agencies for executing American economic imperialism. Perkins joined the international consulting firm, Chas. T. Main, in 1971 as an economist and remained there as an extremely successful EHM until 1980, when his conscience, stricken by what he was doing, compelled him to quit.[89] As Perkins relates, U.S. intelligence agencies would identify prospective EHMs, but they would be hired and paid by international corporations so that their dirty work, if exposed, could be traced back to corporate greed, not to government policy. In his early training, Perkins was told that his job would be to bring leaders of developing countries into the imperial network run by a collection of corporations, banks, and governments. Some of the tools used to accomplish this were fraudulent financial reports, rigged elections, payoffs, and extortion. If the EHM is completely successful, he will have persuaded these developing country leaders to accept loans so large that the debtor nation will default in a few years and have to borrow more, accepting structural adjustments that will make the debtor nation subservient to the U.S., as American operatives demand their votes in the UN, accommodation for military bases, and access to precious resources.[90]

The money for the loans comes from the World Bank, the U.S. Agency for International Development

(USAID), and other similar organizations. What the developing nations' leaders gain is the enhancement of their political position resulting from the infrastructure projects they are able to build with the loans: for example, industrial parks, power plants, airports, and roads. All of the construction must be done by American firms, which reap fabulous profits. Most of the money never leaves the U.S. but moves directly from the offices of the lending agencies to the offices of the American corporations. The developing nations, of course, are left to pay back loan principal and interest.[91]

↣ **Consequences.** I have already described in general terms some of the consequences of globalized economic imperialism. Here I mention several illustrative specific cases.

- In the quest for cheap labor, American companies set up manufacturing operations in Mexico, where marginalized workers had no leverage to bargain for living wages, health care, retirement benefits, or safety standards. One project used primarily adolescent girls whose dexterous fingers enabled them to manipulate tiny production pieces. Minimal working conditions resulted in their loss of eyesight and of physical dexterity, leading to burnout for most of them after five or six years. That the company's profits were earned at the expense of these women's labor, health, and livelihood will never be acknowledged by any corporations or the ideology that supports them.[92]

- In a 2006 speech Bill Moyers reported on how the Mariana Islands, a UN trusteeship administered by the U.S. Interior Department and exempted from U.S. labor and immigration laws, have become both an opulent tourist haven and an American sweatshop. Over the years tens of thousands of immigrants, mainly Chinese women, have been brought to these islands as garment workers to live and work in miserable conditions. They were forbidden to engage in political and religious activities and to socialize or marry. Some of the biggest names in the clothing industry were able to put "made in the U.S.A." labels on the clothes and import them to America while paying the workers virtual slave wages. All efforts to reform these conditions have been rebuffed: after a visit to the islands, Tom Delay pronounced that they represent "what is best about America."[93]

- When John Perkins first visited Ecuador in 1968, just after Texaco had discovered oil there, it was rich in rare animal and plant life. The country contained diverse human cultures, and a number of indigenous languages were spoken along with Spanish. By 2003, a trans-Andean pipeline had leaked over a half million barrels of oil into the fragile rain forest. Vast areas of the forest had fallen—with macaws and jaguars almost extinct, three indigenous cultures on the verge of collapse, and pristine rivers turned into flaming cesspools. As for the economic "benefits," the official poverty level has grown from 50% to 70%, under- or unemployment has risen from 15% to 70%, and the public debt has increased from $240 million to $16 billion. For every $100 of crude oil taken from the rain forests, the oil companies receive $75. Of the remaining $25, $18.75 goes for debt service; most of the remainder covers government expenses, which leaves $2.50 for the health, education, and care of the poor. Thus have the EHMs helped American imperialism turn Ecuador into a typical and "quintessential victim" of economic globalization.[94]

I acknowledge that there are people of high moral resolve who desire to eliminate poverty, yet who are less critical of transnational corporations than are the thinkers I have just discussed. One splendid example is Jeffrey Sachs, who in *The End of Poverty* proposes a plan to end extreme world poverty by 2025. Sachs is somewhat critical of developing countries that have rejected foreign trade and thereby isolated themselves from advancing technology. Their high-cost local industries could not have been competitive even if the nations had chosen to compete. These countries need to increase their exports in order to accumulate foreign exchange, and Sachs points out that countries with open trade have grown more rapidly than countries with closed trade. Moreover, rising per capita incomes in most countries have been associated with a rise in the ratio of trade to gross domestic product.[95] While Sachs admires the moral fervor of the antiglobalists, he disagrees with some of their positions. He acknowledges the bad behavior of some companies, but thinks that the anti-corporate "tirade" is unjustified and based on an uninformed, knee-jerk antipathy to capitalism. In Sachs's view, the opponents of globalization fail to understand that capitalists can support social concerns and accept government interventions in the economy to address unmet needs.[96]

While I agree that anti-globalists should recognize the successes of globalization where they exist, I find Sachs overly optimistic about capitalism "with a human face." He seems not to have taken sufficient account of the multiplied specific instances of damage and suffering caused by globalization. Furthermore, while some capitalists have expressed some willingness to accept some government intervention, this openness has hardly been a leading edge in American capitalism. Moreover, the elimination of government controls has been a primary goal of the structural adjustment loans pressed upon the developing world. We can certainly agree with Sachs that globalists and anti-globalists should join in an enlightened globalization that would put pressure on the rich nations and address the needs of the poorest of the poor.[97]

Taking Stock

I return to the question with which I began this chapter. Have we heard the warning to change to a more just society? If the miscarriage of justice has not been complete, we have, nevertheless, failed in flagrant ways to make appropriate changes for the better, and have in crucial areas made things worse. Our situation may be symbolically epitomized by the government's reaction to a recent intelligence report. According to the assessment made by the nation's most veteran analysts, while the al-Qaeda leadership has been damaged, the threat from Islamic extremists has spread in both numbers and geographic reach. Despite the evidence that the report gives, President Bush and his advisers continue to insist that the Iraqi war has made the world safer.[98] It would seem that this administration cannot recognize reality or speak the truth. This failure exemplifies the affirmation of the Gospel of John that a refusal to accept the light of truth pushes us deeper into the darkness, making it ever harder to recognize the truth.

We stand between warning and consequence. If we have not heeded the warning, what kind of consequence can we expect?

9.

Conclusion:
Dangerous Scenarios and
Hopeful Opportunities

Where Might We Be Headed?

Comparing our situation with the histories of earlier Western empires may offer some illumination regarding the possibilities and probabilities before us.

Kevin Phillips has compared the Spanish, Dutch, and British empires, arguing convincingly that despite variations among them, all three passed through the same stages, from (1) a period of simple beginnings characterized by farming, fishing, and soldiering, through (2) a stage of commerce and industry, and finally into (3) a period dominated by financialization.[1] This last stage is characterized by capital management, excessive debt, great disparity between rich and poor, and general economic decline. Especially noteworthy in this last stage is the development of a large class of people living off of unearned income like interest or rent. Other, non-financial characteristics of this period include problems dealing with natural resources, wars, and excessive expressions of religion. All of these features, Phillips asserts, signal a late time of vulnerability and weakness after which the empire declines.[2]

The similarities between our time and the last phase of these earlier empires are obvious: war, religious extremism, and resource problems (oil). Our debt is enormous, and moving money around occupies a larger share of our gross domestic product than does manufacturing. The proportion of our population living off of unearned income is relatively larger than that of the earlier empires. It would be self-deception indeed to assure ourselves that we will not replicate their failure, for they were all quite confident of their own invincibility.[3]

In our day, three danger-laden scenarios are being played out in a period that resembles the decline of the earlier European empires. For the sake of analysis, I will distinguish the environmental from the economic, but in actuality these two dimensions impact each other powerfully.

→ **Environmental Collapse.** The troubling signs of environmental damage as the result of human behavior are unmistakably evident. Arctic ice and glaciers have been melting during the last two years at a rate ten to fifteen times greater than in the past, resulting in a 20% decrease in the extent of the ice, and the endangerment of the oceanic ecosystem and the lives of marine mammals.[4] Plant and animal species alike have been shifting closer to the poles and higher up mountains; spring is starting earlier in some areas; and in the northern hemisphere, migratory routes of birds have shifted northward. The surface temperature of lakes has risen worldwide as forests have failed; and in the Antarctic, increasingly wide swards of greenery have appeared along with significant reductions in the penguin population. There are many more such indicators. Tim Flannery has warned that it is already too late to avoid unfortunate changes, but that if we act *now* we can prevent disaster.

Otherwise we face an ecological collapse.[5] Failure to act now could seal the fate of hundreds of thousands of species and billions of people. Flannery believe that 50 more years of business-as-usual will make the collapse of civilization inevitable. He demonstrates, for example, the negative effects of climate change on our water and food supplies, with water being the first critical resource to be affected. Imagine, for example, the loss of a city's fresh water supply: no water to drink, wash clothes, or flush toilets. We do not know how much of a temperature change would be required to destroy the networks providing resources to our urban centers, but we should be warned by the knowledge that an increase of 1.1°F has inflicted acute distress in the polar regions.[6]

Jared Diamond has shown how intrinsically connected are the environment and the world economy. The crucial factor affecting survival is not the size of the world's population in itself but the per capita impact we have on our environment—that is, the amount of resources consumed and wastes produced by each person—which varies greatly around the world. On average, each citizen of the U.S., Europe, and Japan consumes 32 times more resources and generates 32 times more waste than does an inhabitant of the developing world. People in the developing world want to rise to developed-world consumption standards, and development agencies encourage this aspiration. Were that to happen, however, for all developing world people, it would mean a twelve-fold increase in the environmental impact of those populations, an impact the world could not sustain. Jared Diamond poses the implicit threat as a question: What will happen when it finally dawns on people in the developing world that developed-world standards are unreachable for them, and that we in the developed world refuse to abandon those standards for ourselves?[7]

➔ Economic Collapse. I will simply list several troubling signs: the magnitude of our national, corporate, and personal debt; high rates of personal consumption and low rates of savings; the loss of our manufacturing base; uncertainty about how long foreign banks will continue to lend to us; our failure to educate young people in math, science, and engineering.[8] Furthermore, our trade deficit continues to augment our debt and to cause a devaluation of the dollar, a situation that resists change because we want many things the Chinese, make but have little to offer them in return.[9] We do not really know when worldwide oil production will peak and begin to decline: our present voracious demand for oil generates problems, as do the increasing difficulties in extracting oil from the earth.[10] Between 2000 and 2004, mortgage debt in the U.S. rose from $4.4 trillion to $7.5 trillion.

Kevin Phillips estimates that the fallout from a 10% to 20% price slump in the national housing market could produce bankruptcies and shattered credit that would put millions of people in a situation comparable to indentured servitude. A recent news report reveals that major building contractors are experiencing reduced sales and profits while the inventory of unsold existing homes is at a thirteen-year high.[11]

What is ahead? Kevin Phillips envisions not so much a cataclysmic disintegration as an economic decline, similar to the adjustments made by the Spanish, Dutch, and British empires after they passed their zenith. China may become the leading world economic power as we approach the mid-21st century.[12] James Fallows's speculative essay, presenting our history from 2001 to 2016, is frighteningly plausible.[13] Fallows writes, in imaginative retrospect, that the tax cuts of 2001 set the stage for economic trouble, but the event that triggered an economic meltdown came in 2009 when Venezuelan President Hugo Chávez defeated an attempted right-wing coup which he blamed on the CIA. Chávez then declared economic war on the U.S., cutting off oil shipments to us but giving China preferential treatment. In the next week, the price of oil in the U.S. increased by 40%, sparking rising interest rates, shrinking businesses, falling stock and bond prices, and soaring gas prices (finally $9 per gallon). The airlines collapsed into a single monopoly; Toyota acquired Ford and General Motors. But nothing matched the nightmare of home foreclosures as millions of evictees moved into RVs and mobile homes, built in idled automobile factories and planted in villages in decommissioned military bases. In Fallows's scenario, half of American households live on less than $50,000 per year, which sounds encouraging—until we read that a private college costs $83,000 a year; a day in a hospital, $1,350; and a year in a nursing home, $150,000.

→ **The Unheeded Slide toward Fascism.** In his important book, *The Anatomy of Fascism*, Robert Paxton cautions that to understand the rise of 20th-century Fascism we should focus not on dramatic events such as the Reichstag fire or *Kristallnacht*, but rather on the complicity of ordinary people without which Fascist movements could not have grown.[14] In 1928, the Nazis won less than 3% of the popular vote, and never won a majority; but in 1932 they became the largest party in the German parliament, with 37.2% of the vote. Between 1928 and 1932, a common front emerged composed of conservative intellectuals, corporate chiefs, politicians, and church leaders. After President Hindenburg appointed Adolf Hitler chancellor in January, 1933, the Nazis briefly governed in coalition with conservatives, gaining a certain respectability from the alliance, while the conservatives gained a popular base and a share in government without having to form a coalition with the Left. The conservative elite believed, wrongly, that they could tame and use the Nazis in order to achieve their own anti-democratic ends. In various ways they were complicit in the Nazi rise to power.[15]

Early on, Hitler learned the value of using God-talk to describe Germany's calling. In his first radio address, he declared his intention to preserve and defend Christianity as the foundation of German national morality. Fritz Stern, a prominent historian of modern Germany, concludes that it was the pseudo-religious transformation of politics that largely ensured Hitler's success.[16]

In earlier chapters I have mentioned troubling signs in American society, most notably the development of an imperial presidency, the erosion of civil liberties, and the advanced technology for massive internal surveillance. Comparative studies on Fascist periods in different nations, including Paxton's work, allow us to identify common recognizable patterns of national behavior and the abuse of power characteristic of Fascism:[17]

> powerful and continuing expressions of nationalism: flags, pins, slogans; > a sense of crisis beyond the reach of traditional solutions; > disdain for the importance of human rights; > a primary group that on one hand sees itself as a victim, threatened by liberalism and alien influences, whose victimization justifies any action, and that on the other hand sees itself as a chosen people with a right to dominate others without restraint; > the identification of enemies and scapegoats as a unifying cause; > the declared need for an authoritative "natural" leader whose instincts are superior to abstract and universal reason; > the supremacy of the military; > rampant sexism, including anti-feminist, anti-abortion, and homophobic sentiments and policies; > a mass media controlled by threats, economic pressure, and appeals to patriotism; > an obsession with national security; > the representation of fervent religiosity on the part of the ruling elite; > protection for corporate power and > the

suppression or elimination of labor power; → disdain for and suppression of intellectuals and the arts; → obsession with crime and punishment; → rampant cronyism and corruption; → fraudulent elections, including elite control of election machinery, intimidation of opposition voters, destruction or disallowance of legal votes, and the resort to a judiciary beholden to the power elite.

Most of these characteristics of Fascism are manifest in American society, to some degree, today. Learning the painful lesson that the passivity and miscalculation of the German people and their conservative leaders made possible the rise of Nazism means that we must heed, understand, and resist these characteristics in our own society today. I have described the consequences of ecological and economic trouble as "collapse," but with regard to incipient Fascism the potential consequence is not so much a cataclysmic explosion or disintegration as a paralyzing constriction. Given the technology now available for surveillance and control, if we allow these present tendencies to continue and intensify, the rule of an imperial president would be, as Senator Frank Church put it, total tyranny.

As I indicated in Chapter 6, my discussion of these troubling scenarios has been informed by Isaiah's configuration of a historical process in which instances of injustice and harm intrinsic in human history culminate in disaster. I have relied, however, on thinkers who make penetrating use of a similar configuration though ordinarily without bringing in the theological horizon. They are *non*-theological witnesses to the power of the prophetic understanding of history. It is, I propose, the task of the theological interpreter of Scripture to think God and history together, to contextualize this segment of American history by suggesting that God is the hidden power directing this process (though, as I have explained above, asserting this does not nullify human interests, motives, or freedom).

What Changes Should We Make?

We should be aware that these three scenarios are not mutually exclusive. For one of these scenarios to culminate in disaster does not mean that we have avoided the others! On the other hand, none of these possible disasters is inevitable, if we have the courage and will to act.

We face a significant challenge internationally: the United States has lost the respect, admiration, and support of most of the rest of the world, and has drawn implacable hatred (which spawns terroristic intentions) from much of the Muslim world. Commentators on this situation have given diametrically opposed answers to the questions, *Why do "they" hate us?* and, *Would changes on our part do any good?* The commentator usually takes an either/or approach.

On one side we hear that we have done nothing to deserve such hatred, but that "they" hate us *because of who we are*, a free and open society. Changing our policies and actions, therefore, would *not* do any good, nor *should* we change what we are.[18] This position probably does describe why some Muslims hate us, and they are not likely to be placated by changes on our part. But it certainly does not account for all animosity toward the U.S. To paraphrase a question that Osama bin Laden posed to George Bush, *If we attack you because you are a free and open society, why are we not attacking, say, Sweden?*[19]

On the other side, we hear that "they" do in fact hate us because of what we have *done*. My discussion of American imperialism in its political, military, and economic aspects shows that there are ample reasons for this hatred. Policies and actions can be modified and reversed, however, and while the damage done is too great to be overcome quickly, substantial changes in our behavior can begin to restore peace and friendly relationships. Our national posture can be different from the one that provoked such hostility. It is this second approach, then, that I believe should carry more weight, precisely because it can do more good.

I have argued from the beginning that all human beings have access to the biblical understanding of justice and are accountable for enacting it. Thus it is not theologically inappropriate to call on a secular nation to repent, in the sense of augmenting the scope of justice. Such repentance does not require a conversion to Christianity.

I do not claim here to set forth a systematic or comprehensive program for actualizing national repentance. But I offer here a number of possibilities for change, identified by various thinkers, that I regard as helpful and ameliorative—and, at least, certainly worthy of our consideration. Most of these changes, in both domestic and international affairs, are structural in nature and must be carried out by domestic and international governments or economic agencies. But we as individual citizens have the responsibility to become informed and to support, in whatever ways we can, those proposals that seem most promising for extending the reach of justice. For us who are Christians, the task is to support policies that most closely approximate biblical social justice. And, as we will see, there are things that individuals can do.

Fairness, Cooperation, and Giving Away While Still Having

Justice as Fairness (John Rawls)

I pointed out in Chapter 5 that for Rawls, justice in a secular, pluralistic democracy should be based on political action and not on religion or metaphysics, and that it should show a preferential concern for the least advantaged. This means that justice should maintain society as a fair system of social cooperation that is efficient and productive over time. *Fairness* requires that people who are similar in all relevant respects should be treated similarly. *Cooperation* requires rules and procedures that are publicly known and regarded as just; reciprocity entails that all who do their part according to the rules benefit according to the rules and that each person has a rational advantage, a good to seek.[20] A fair system of distributive justice would supply what free and equal citizens are entitled to, by providing income and wealth sufficient to achieve a wide range of goals. Such a system would ensure the social basis of self-respect essential for citizens to have a lively sense of their self-worth and to achieve their goals with self-confidence.[21]

According to Rawls, our present system is a "welfare-state capitalism" that allows a relatively few people to control the economic and political order. Though it aims to keep any people from falling below a decent minimum standard of life, this system has allowed an underclass to develop and has not addressed this underclass through a redistribution of income until it is too late: thus we have a discouraged and depressed underclass chronically dependent on welfare. Rawls prefers "property-owning democracy," which seeks to prevent the development of an underclass in the first place and to restrain the monopolistic control of economic and political life by a small segment of society. Moreover, such a democracy undertakes a greater dispersal of the ownership of wealth and capital by developing *human capital*, through education and training, by employing the inheritance tax, and by means of government intervention and control of the free market in order to prevent excessive inequality in the distribution of wealth.[22]

Rawls concedes that our political culture is not ready for such a property-owning democracy at the present time.[23] I nevertheless believe the material continuity between the concern of biblical justice for "the most vulnerable" and the Rawlsian preference for "the least advantaged" makes his vision an important one for us to continue to lift up before our society—the very society for which Rawls articulated it.

The Cooperative Society (Kathryn Tanner)

Kathryn Tanner discusses the prospects for a cooperative, rather than competitive, society. She begins from a theological question: What if God offers us the world and the goods of life—all that we need—as a totally gracious, unconditional gift (seen first in creation, in which God gives everything before we could have done anything), and expects us to organize and structure society so as to extend these goods absolutely inclusively, in such a way as to reflect the character of God's giving?[24]

Tanner distinguishes subtly between *receiving* God's gifts and *responding* to them. Although we do nothing to merit *receiving* these gifts, *responding* to them requires doing something to make them a part of our lives. However, Tanner can also speak of receipt and response as if they are the same thing, a tension I will not pursue here.[25] Tanner mentions the progressive income tax as one way to redistribute wealth, reduce inequality, and thus provide everyone the benefit of living in a more uniformly well-off populace. This is one example, she argues, of how some (wealthier members of society) might relinquish income without having their economic life go down the drain (as is the current experience of the poor). That is, one can give away and still have at the same time. How is this possible?[26]

The New Testament

Several New Testament texts are pertinent to our consideration of the sorts of public-policy proposals that Rawls and Tanner name, because they deal with theological, existential, and social organization issues. Matthew attests to the reality of unconditional grace in nature. Paul describes the faith that responds to such grace in both nature and history. Mark lays out the kind of social restructuring that enables believers to give away their wealth radically.

1. Grace and Freedom from Anxiety in the Gospel of Matthew. Matthew offers the basis for a just and cooperative economy in the continuing creative activity of God in nature. In the last antithesis in the Sermon on the Mount (Matt 5:43-48), Matthew's Jesus opposes his teaching on love for enemies to the hatred of enemies that (in his view) the Jewish tradition requires. The model for the disciples' love for the enemy as well as the friend is God's gracious, non-discriminating love for all human beings, which is expressed through the bounty of nature: God makes the sun rise and the rain fall—the sources of life and well-being in the world—on both the righteous and the unrighteous, without regard for merit or deserving. God's non-discriminating love shapes both the *norm* of the love of enemies (5:48) and the *reason* for obeying the norm (5:44-45). But more, this saying describes God's unmerited love by means of the creation's continuing beneficent support for socioeconomic life; the command to love, therefore, also refers inescapably to the particular responsibility to provide for the well-being of others in the public economic order.

Another passage, Matt 6:25-34, helps us to interpret the first one. In the second, Jesus exhorts his hearers not to be anxious about food and clothing. We are inevitably anxious, however, if we imagine that our goal in life is the security that accumulated wealth might give us, yet recognize, even dimly, that such accumulation is finally beyond our control. Jesus calls his hearers to trust instead in God and to seek God's kingdom ("Do not be anxious"). "Consider the birds of the air and the lilies of the field," Jesus says they do no work, and apparently suffer no anxiety, yet God cares for them bountifully through the workings of nature. As we have seen, God also cares for humans by means of nature's non-discriminating benefits (5:43-48), but this does not mean that human beings may simply stop working (much less that we may stop striving to achieve a more just social order). The exhortation is not to give up work but to renounce anxiety and trust God to provide what is needed—by means, I suggest, of both the natural *and historical-social* orders. Human beings belong to a different order from animals and flowers, an order of "much more" (6:25-26, 30): If God cares for forms of life that do not work, *how much more* will God care for the needs (6:32) of the human order in which people *do* work! Yet because of the human tendency to serve wealth rather than God (Matt. 6:24), Gods gracious intention does not always work: the beneficence of the natural order is deformed, the basic needs of many remain unfulfilled; and therefore we must work to achieve justice.

2. Paul: Justification by faith—theological and social. Here I am amplifying a position toward which Elsa Támez points in her discussion of Martin Luther.[27] For Luther (and, I would add, for Paul), the gift of *justification* addresses those who are uncertain of salvation because their consciences condemn them for a lack of good works

toward God. Justification assures people that God accepts them despite a lack of meritorious works. How does this translate into the socioeconomic realm? I believe we should translate the theological principle of *justification* into a principle of *social justice*. That is, the gift of *justice* addresses those who are anxious and uncertain because their lack of economically productive achievements has marginalized them and rendered them insignificant. *Justice* assures them that their bodily and material needs will be satisfied and accords them dignity despite their lack of economic power.

But what is the source of this practice of justice? How are those who have experienced justification in the theological sense enabled and prompted to enact the kind of social justice (the satisfaction of needs) that I have just suggested?

For Paul, the light of the gospel shines in our hearts to reveal Christ to us (2 Cor. 4:6), but also to make us see our own hidden purposes (1 Cor. 4:5; 14:25). Whether or not our own conscience condemns us for what we see, our right relationship with God depends on God's judgment (1 Cor. 4:4-5). God does not count merits, but rather acquits the guilty (Rom. 3:21-25; 4:5; Phil. 3:8-10). Since God accepts us, no other condemnation of us counts (Rom. 8:33-39). Since God does not deal with us on the basis of our own moral righteousness, we are freed from the compulsive but impossible task of trying to establish our own righteousness and from trying to conceal our failure. Being delivered from this concentration upon ourselves, we are free to embrace the totality of reality (1 Cor. 3:21-23), free even to relinquish our freedom for the well-being of the other (1 Cor. 9:19-23). We can dispose ourselves toward our neighbor for his or her advantage, not for our own (Rom. 15:1-2; 1 Cor. 10:24, 33; 1 Thess. 5:15; Phil. 2:4). *This* is what makes it possible for us to enact in the social realm what we have experienced in the divine-human transaction of justification.

3. The Rich man's encounter with Jesus in the Gospel of Mark. This story (Mark 10:17-31) offers a picture of a social situation in which the individual can give radically to others without having his or her own economic life disintegrate. A rich man comes to Jesus seeking eternal life; then Jesus discusses with his disciples the difficulty of the rich being saved. We should note that the story portrays the rich man in a favorable light. He initiates the moment of possibility by approaching Jesus, praising and honoring him, and asking what he must do to inherit eternal life. He knows that he is both rich and morally upright, and Jesus takes him at his word and loves him (Mark 10:19-20). Jesus does not accuse him of being self-righteous nor suggest that his wealth rendered him hard and callous. The rich man is aware of the reality of God, and knows that something is missing in his life: Wealth and moral achievement have not given him eternal life, and he wants to know how to find it. When Jesus tells him that the way to eternal life is through obedience to God's moral commandments, he replies that he has offered this to God since his youth. Again, Jesus takes him at his word—but tells him that he lacks one thing, which apparently is everything. He will have treasure in heaven if he sells what he has and gives the money to the poor, then follows Jesus.

Hearing this, the man's face darkened, and he went away grieving and distressed because he had many possessions. Why did it end this way? Why does he hold onto his wealth rather than lay hold on eternal life?

We can discern three intertwined reasons. First and most obviously, the rich man simply wants the security and, possibly, the pleasure that his wealth offers. Second, however, he also lacks the power to make the radical move required of him. Though he wants eternal life—this is what brought him to Jesus in the first place, and he is shocked and grieved to see it slipping away—some stronger power apparently drives him to go against his own best intention: as the parable of the sower suggests (Mark 4:19), the deceptiveness of wealth has lured him away from his best intention, has choked it out of him.

Two aphoristic sayings of Jesus from Matthew provide a revealing theological context for interpreting this aspect of the rich man's refusal. In the first (Matt. 6:21), Jesus says that our hearts will be attached to what we treasure: our understanding of the world and our ability to act in it will be oriented to either earthly or heavenly treasures. In the second saying (Matt. 6:24), the choice is between serving either God or wealth as lord or master (*kyrios*), with the power to demand service and determine our lives. Because each requires total and exclusive devotion, serving both is quite impossible. Paul Tillich interpreted such biblical language by declaring that authentic religion is ultimate concern about God, the power and ground of being. Ultimate concern means loving God alone, with all of our being and without reservation.[28] But we can, and do, attribute ultimacy to what is only preliminary, less than God, and unable to save us. By over-valuing a finite reality we thus create it as our functional god, really a demonic power, against which we make ourselves powerless.[29] The wealth from which we expect salvation and ultimate security becomes a demonic god that controls our lives destructively.

The value of the story of the rich man in Mark is that it describes a crisis of self-discovery. Most of us are familiar with the biblical requirement that we worship only God (Mark 12:28-30). We readily convince ourselves that we in fact do *worship* and serve God alone, and simply *use* our wealth (ideally, of course, for worthy purposes). This story confronts us (as Jesus confronted the rich man) with the question, where are we, really, in relation to God and money? The turn comes when we (like the rich man) realize that we have really been worshiping wealth, when all along we thought that we were worshiping God. The veil of self-deception is torn away and we get a shocking glimpse of what we have actually been doing. We confront a decision: will we continue in the same direction, or begin to live out a radically different story? The rich man in the story discovered that he could not make the break: faced with a decision, he found he could not give up his wealth, even in order to have eternal life—which he had thought he wanted. We face a similar decision. It is facing the call to surrender our wealth voluntarily for the sake of the poor—and for the sake of our own eternal life—that reveals what we really worship.

We may imagine a third reason for the rich man's failure: the legitimate fear that if he gives all his wealth away, he may become destitute, dependent on others, and perhaps unable to care for the lives and well-being of his family. It is the practical legitimacy of this fear that may limit the story's validity for us. In itself it penetratingly represents the crisis of the individual who is called upon to take a drastic economic risk, but it does not deal with wider structural dimensions of poverty. It provides no answer to the question: *If* I give up my wealth for the sake of the poor, what assures me of some reciprocal benefit? What will protect me and my family from destitution?

Here Jesus' subsequent conversation with his disciples about whether the rich can be saved (10:23-27) is of particular importance. If even a small amount of wealth can become the false object of ultimate concern, it is impossible for human beings to be saved: they lack the spiritual and moral resources to give up their attachment to whatever they mistakenly believe can make them secure. But all things are possible with God. God saves by giving the kind of faith that entails freedom *from* self-interest and freedom *for* God and the other person. And God saves *by providing a new kind of community, a social restructuring that makes it possible for an individual to dispense his or her wealth radically without becoming destitute.* In Mark, God's transformation of Jesus' death into the victory of resurrection life (8:31; 9:31; 10:33-34, 45) offers his followers a paradoxical way of participating in the movement from death to life. At an existential level, this participation means we gain our authentic selves by risking our hardened and deformed self-interested selves (8:34-37). At the level of personal ethics, we become "Number One" by being servant of all (9:35; 10:43-44). And at the level of social ethics, we make a hundredfold gain of houses, fields, mothers, sisters, brothers, and children precisely by giving up those very same things that are individually ours (10:29-31).

Jesus asks the rich man to give up his wealth to the poor, but in the larger Markan context, the poor are other members of the community, who have become poor by giving the community their wealth. No one in the community really becomes or remains poor by doing so, because each individual is sustained by the wealth of all. There is no private property: all are supported by the new commonwealth.

We will not begin to reduce the gulf between the rich and the poor in our society without replacing an absolute value on private property with the biblical concept of property, where ownership is relative to the needs of others (see Chapter 2). Nothing in the texts we have considered suggests that each person or family should receive equal income from the common wealth, nor do I suppose a modern economy oriented to such a standard is necessarily desirable; such a standard would ignore the great differences among individuals regarding intelligence, skills, energy, imagination, and the will to work, and would violate the justice principle of proportionality between contribution and compensation.

Jesus' encounter with the rich man does, however, suggest a system of distributive justice oriented toward meeting the basic needs of all, domestically and globally. To apply the challenge to the rich man in political terms appropriate to our context: are we prepared to support a rigorously progressive tax system and other government interventions necessary to provide universal, affordable, and competent health care, safe and comfortable housing, good schools in every part of town, and income adequate to participate fully in communal life? Are we prepared to establish a poverty line below which no person or family would be allowed to fall, to ensure that all of these, and other comparable needs, are met? Are we prepared to establish legislation limiting the gap between those just above the poverty line and the richest of the rich?

An economy organized to reflect God's unconditional giving would distribute society's goods without concern for whether the recipients were "deserving." It would protect the well-being of all without exception. But how, practically speaking, can people be expected to give in this unconditional, selfless way without some expectation of reciprocity? The thought of organizing such an economy seems wild and unworkable because we have not experienced anything like it.[30] To move toward such an economy, we would all need to embrace two convictions: first, that all people have a common right to what they need (a conviction that follows immediately from the Christian knowledge of God's unconditional, giving love to all God's creatures); and second, that possessing property need not be exclusive and competitive. My possessing something need not mean it is not also another's, and my giving something to another need not mean it ceases to be mine. Giving to others and having for oneself are not mutually exclusive, as our Markan text shows. In a noncompetitive form of possession, everyone can continue to benefit from what he or she gives to others.[31]

Moving toward a More Participatory Economy

One way to curb the excessive power of corporations and to democratize corporate governance is to shift from shareholder to stakeholder capitalism. Justice requires that all who are affected by the policies or actions of an institution should participate in its governance. Stakeholders in a particular business include external agencies such as suppliers, customers, government, and the local community. Internal stakeholders would include boards of directors, employees, and unions, as well as shareholders. In this view, shareholders are not the only stakeholders, and profit is not the sole determiner of policy. Corporations exist to create wealth for the whole of society; thus all who have a stake in the operation should have a role in decision-making.[32]

The principle of stakeholder capitalism should be extended into the global economy so that developing countries especially would become stakeholders in transnational corporations. This would mean that the voices of the marginalized would be heard and their cultures respected as interaction between corporations and communities is increased. Many in the developing world call for smaller economies and a shift away from mass-produced food and consumer products. They resist international leveling, and push for the restoration of local production for local consumption rather than for export. (The case of Ghana, where the colonial imposition of cocoa production for export devastated the local economy and also the stability of the Ashanti people, is an example.[33])

Some citizens of the developing world see themselves as colonies in a new colonialism and believe that the transnational corporations will not relinquish their privileged position voluntarily, but must be compelled, either by political action on the part of postcolonialists of the developing world, or by a critical collapse of the world economic system. They see a need for hundreds of economic, social, and political resistance networks to enable them to reclaim their sovereign rights over the transnational corporations and banks. They are fighting for their rights to adequate food, clothing, shelter, employment, education, health care, a clean environment, social equality, public services, and self-determination.[34] For the most part, these postcolonialists want to maintain the freedom of movement and capital, but they also want to make their own decisions. Their goal is smaller, localized economies, connected with but not dominated by outside forces.[35]

The absolute necessity of growth has been a primary doctrine of corporate behavior: an extreme expression of this position was the pronouncement of Lawrence Summers, former Harvard president, that it would be a profound error to put limits on growth because of some supposed natural limit.[36] Others have been more cautious, insisting that we must limit growth to a dimension that our ecosystem can in fact sustain—thus the formula "sustainable growth." But others have gone further. Jerry Mander has argued that exponential economic growth—economies built for export trade rather than local needs, and continued emphasis on commodity accumulation—cannot be sustained beyond a very short time.[37] Herman Daly reminds us that the economy is a subsystem of the earth's ecosystem, which is finite, nongrowing, and materially closed, which means that economic growth is not infinitely sustainable. The term "sustainable growth," applied to the economy, is thus an oxymoron: the economy can develop, change, be transformed, or be qualitatively improved, but it cannot get bigger.[38]

If the economy cannot grow forever, can it still grow enough to give everyone in the world a standard of per capita resource use equal to that of the average American? Even that would require the economy's growth by a factor of seven. The available evidence about global warming, acid rain, and other ecological indicators shows that the present scale of growth is *already* unsustainable. An increase by a factor of seven would turn unsustainability into imminent collapse. What we must accomplish is *qualitative* development that would provide food, clothing, and shelter (but not luxury consumption) for all, along with population control and wealth redistribution.[39]

Peter Singer argues that in order to achieve the kind of goals I have been discussing we must have an international agency with the authority to set international standards and regulations and the power to enforce them. He suggests that the WTO might be reformed to become such an agency.[40]

Reversing American Imperialism

Here I will present several points of view.

European historians Vassilis Fouskas and Bülent Gokay have a succinct proposal for resolving the conflict with Islamic terrorism. "Anglo-Saxon" power should be withdrawn from the greater

Middle East; the Israeli army should withdraw from the West Bank and Gaza; and the foundation for an independent Palestinian state should be laid. Then Islam and the West could explore how to establish a democratic and *civilian* structure of political and economic cooperation based on mutual respect and understanding.[41]

The American Ivan Eland (a moderate liberal, and a "realist" on foreign policy) maintains that Americans should clearly identify our truly vital interests and defend them—but only them—vigorously. We should do whatever is necessary to secure our foreign trade, but should limit our geopolitical concerns to North America, Europe, and East Asia. Eland clearly believes in a balance-of-power international politics. He holds that the U.S. should engage in war only to prevent a destruction of "balance," which means that we should fight to prevent any potential hegemon from taking over any of the three areas in which we have vital interests. But the Middle East and its oil, Eland insists, are *not* within our sphere of vital interests.[42] Eland recommends actions that are radical compared to our present projects. The U.S. should terminate all formal and informal alliances; withdraw all our armed forces based overseas; convert to a smaller but highly efficient military that can project power from the U.S.; cut our massive defense budget by a little more than half; and maintain a reduced nuclear arsenal as an ultimate deterrent. His reasons: our present policy of alliances and military bases has costs that outweigh its benefits; it is foolish; it tends to draw us into unwanted wars; and it provokes more terrorism.[43] Eland denies that his position is isolationist. He advocates free commerce, a liberal immigration policy, and diplomatic and cultural exchanges among nations (for example, with China: Eland assigns our suspicion of China to our "need" to have an enemy now that Russia is no longer a real rival, and proposes we grant China's desire to have its legitimate regional sphere of influence).[44]

Andrew Bacevich (a West Point graduate, Vietnam veteran; a cultural conservative, distinguished scholar, yet an acute critic of American militarism and the Bush administration) argues that the American people need to undergo a change of consciousness. We must renounce the assumption that military action is the normal and only real alternative for addressing international conflicts, and our government must reaffirm the (apparently lost) Constitutional principles that the military's purpose is to provide for our common defense, not to project American power throughout the world or remake the world in our image. The excessive power in any branch of the government is to be checked by the separation of powers. Only the Congress has the constitutional power to "declare war." We must restrain the inordinate tendency of the executive to engage in war in order to extend our security borders;[45] we must bring home troops stationed abroad, except where there is an immediate need for their presence; and we should greatly reduce the size of our military and the magnitude of defense spending.[46]

Robert Cooper (a distinguished British diplomat-scholar) compares modern and postmodern theories of international relations, and calls for a move toward the postmodern. The modern state system, beginning with the Peace of Westphalia (1648), was defined by the theory of a balance of power between opposing blocs and assumed that, given the balance, neither side would take the risk of attacking the other; the theory aimed at preventing both continuous wars and the rise of a single hegemonic power. The theory also assumed that each nation was sovereign with borders impervious to interference from other nations, and that each nation maintained a monopoly of force within its borders. Since the underlying assumption is one of enmity, force is the ultimate guarantor of security; each nation must keep secret its actual military position. Cooper sees the U.S. as a "robustly modern" state, much less open than the European countries to interdependence, openness, mutual surveillance, and mutual interference.[47] By contrast, the postmodern system, which emerged in 1989 with the founding of the European Union, spelled the end of balance-of-power politics in Europe and of the imperial impulse. No longer do the European countries want to fight each other. Force is no longer an option for settling disputes; it must be replaced by a framework of law, bargaining, and arbitration. Impervious borders have been replaced by mutual interference in each other's domestic affairs and constraints on each other's monopoly of force. Transparency has replaced secrecy, as each state must inform the others (for example) of the location of conventional heavy weapons. Cooper recognizes that a large-scale movement toward this position is a long-term vision, but remarks that it will not do just to wait and hope.[48]

Michael Ignatieff observes a widespread agreement that the UN needs to be strengthened, and suggests some ways in which the U.S. could take the lead by reforming the Security Council, where the problems lie.[49] He suggests enlarging the number of Security Council permanent members to reflect the geopolitical situation today, asking why Britain and France are permanent members but nations such as India, Germany, and Brazil are not. He suggests that the U.S. give up its UN Security Council veto in the hope other nations would follow suit; that the Security Council should make decisions to use force by a simple majority; that the U.S. should commit to use force only with the Council's approval unless our national security is directly threatened; and that the U.S. should prioritize defense of civil rights above defending national sovereignty at all costs. To accomplish the last, Ignatieff suggests the U.S. lead by proposing in the UN that intervention in sovereign states be approved to prevent ethnic cleansing and mass killing; to restore a democracy that has been overthrown when people inside the state ask for help; to reverse the violation of nonproliferation protocols regarding WMDs; to force a state to cease allowing terrorists on its own soil to launch attacks on other countries; or to help a state that is a victim of aggression when that state calls for help. Ignatieff doubts that these reforms are possible, but judges that the UN has no future without them. The alternative to reform is a muddled, lurching American empire, policing an ever more resistant world and being sabotaged by former allies.

Environmental Protection

Flannery has proposed a set of changes with regard to the environment: The U.S. must reduce

CO_2 emissions by 70% by 2050, which requires beginning to decarbonize the electricity grids by 2030 and substantially decarbonizing the transportation systems by 2050. A variety of non-fossil energy sources is available—including wind, solar, nuclear, and ethanol—and all of them must be employed. Flannery says the most important thing government could do would be to ban the building or expansion of coal-fired power plants.[50] Both Flannery and Peter Singer have suggested the establishment of international institutions with power to enforce the requirements of international law and to limit national sovereignty.[51] Flannery warns against the remote but perilous possibility that an Orwellian-style world government could be established, with power to control every inch of our planet, as a necessity to ensure our very survival if we delay voluntary action to combat the climate crisis.[52] Jared Diamond holds that the primary obstacle to undertaking any of these steps has been cost. In certain circumstances, Diamond observes, a business may maximize its profits in the short run by damaging the environment and hurting people, but he argues it is too easy to condemn business alone: corporations have an obligation to their shareholders to maximize profits, so long as they do it legally. I would question the dominance that that obligation has acquired stakeholder capitalism is a fairer alternative to profit-dominated shareholder capitalism. But Diamond is right: the public bears responsibility for allowing business to profit by hurting people and the environment, for example, by buying wood products from non-sustainable logging operations. We should act (directly and through our elected representatives) to reward companies that protect the environment and punish companies that damage it.[53]

Finally, Gregg Easterbrook argues that although past successes in protecting and restoring the environment have been easier and cheaper than anticipated, we now seem overwhelmed by a paralyzing pessimism, a listless fatalism, regarding environmental problems. We need to recast the challenge in practical, optimistic terms, and we need leaders to move us to action.[54]

Specific Action Proposals

In light of these proposals, there are many things that we as individuals can do.

Congress and the Supreme Court should assume their Constitutional responsibilities to restrain the executive branch's violations of civil liberties. And individuals must live out their freedoms—to speak, to write, to protest—lest these precious, hard-won freedoms wither away. The government will gladly move into any vacuum we create by failing to act.

Individuals can act on behalf of the environment by being careful about electricity use, looking for green-power options, using solar power for heat and hot water, and using energy-efficient cars and appliances.[55]

To constrain greed and reduce gross economic inequality, Peter Singer[56] suggests that individuals in affluent societies give at least 1% of their income to those who lack sufficient food, clean water, shelter from the elements, and basic health care. John Perkins[57] urges us to downsize our homes, wardrobes, cars, offices, and other aspects of our lives, and that we protest free-market capitalism and sweatshop exploitation.

Rebecca Peters[58] proposes the formation of affectional communities that can overcome isolation, promote social relations and public policy, and help neutralize the business and governmental sectors that determine so much of our present policy. We can examine our consumption patterns and consider what we might do together to limit the power and wealth of the richest of the rich, who depend upon our habits of consumption. But we should not imagine that all of the guilt and responsibility lie with the very rich. As many as 1.3 billion people in the world live on less than $1 (U.S.) per day; the median U.S. income is $42,400. Many of us bear responsibility to make things different.

Conclusion

At the end of Chapter 1, I set out Jack Forstman's searching questions: Will the Christian tradition enable us to recognize demonic evil before it becomes boldly entrenched? Will it give us the courage to name that evil publicly and say "no" to it? In Part 2, I have discussed judgment as the culminating explosion of a disintegrative process that occurs within the unfolding of our national stories. Making the policy and action changes suggested here would begin to address those questions.

We ought to make these changes on both the domestic and international fronts (1) because it is God who has stamped the world with justice and enjoined all of God's human creatures to reflect that justice, (2) because it would confer benefits upon the victims of injustice, and (3) because it is in our self-interest to do so. If we reshape society justly, we may avert the eruption of inequality and division into anarchy and chaos. We cannot be certain that our self-interested intentions will be realized. While we have reason to believe that reforms in the administration of justice will improve the lives of millions of people and begin to resolve dangerous conflicts, we do not have mastery over consequences we neither intend nor anticipate. That uncertainty is even more intense on the international front. While we might hope that those who oppose us because of our actions will be pacified by policy changes on our part, we know there are also those who oppose us for what we are, and they may well attack again. As Robert Cooper observes, despite the fact that the U.S. holds unrestrainable military hegemony and therefore that no nation or alliance is likely to attack us in a conventional nation-state war, there may well be individuals or nations that will be attracted to unconventional means (as on 9/11). We might find ourselves in the ironical situation of being the only military power that counts, yet at the same time subject to continuous terrorist attacks—both all-powerful and all-vulnerable.[59] From a prudential light, we should not languish in pursuing the self-interested aspect of improving and saving lives, both of others and our own, for the history of empires offers us a lesson that is neither sanguine nor consoling. Despite any failure, however, to reach our self-interested goals, we ought to make changes to enlarge the scope of justice because of the first two reasons given above.

We should make these changes out of recognition of the biblical God, who is the first and the last, who holds the whole of nature and history, who purposes to do new things that we have not dreamed of and whose purposes cannot be thwarted (Isa. 42:9; 43:13, 19; 46:13; 48:6-8, 12-13). This God can turn even our intentions to do harm into life-saving benefits (Gen. 45:5-8; 50:20). For Paul, this is the God who brings life out of death, reality out of nothingness (Rom. 4:16-25). We participate in this God's projects through faith, interpreted as expectant hope, neither contingent nor conditional—hope that risks commitment to a venture whose outcome hardly seems certain, yet hope in God's promise of life in the face of death and the impossible. We should pursue change that will extend the scope of justice, trying to imagine the extraordinary uses to which God might put our intentions and actions—compromised though they may be.

Notes

Chapter 1

1. Jack Forstman, *Christian Faith in Dark Times* (Louisville: Westminster/John Knox, 1992), 20.

Chapter 2

1. E. Clinton Gardner, *Justice and Christian Ethics* (Cambridge: University Press, 1998), 22.

2. The Aristotle references are to Aristotle, *The Nicomachean Ethics*, The Loeb Classical Library (Cambridge, Mass.: Harvard University Press (1994). In the following the abbreviation *NE* will be used for *The Nichomachean Ethics*.

3. Bruce C. Birch, *Let Justice Roll Down* (Louisville: Westminster/John Knox, 1991), 155; Bruce V. Malchow, *Social Justice in the Hebrew Bible* (Collegeville, Minn.: Liturgical Press, 1996), 16-17.

4. Walter Brueggemann, *Theology of the Old Testament* (Minneapolis: Fortress Press, 1997), 736-7; Gardner, *Justice*, 45-6.

5. Brueggemann, *Theology*, 736-9.

6. Klaus Koch, "Is There a Doctrine of Retribution in the Old Testament?" in *Theodicy in the Old Testament*, ed. J. Crenshaw (Philadelphia: Fortress Press, 1983), 59, 74.

7. Ibid., 60-69, 74.

8. Brueggemann, *Theology*, 119-25, 135.

9. David M. Carr, *The Erotic Word* (Oxford: Oxford University Press, 2003), 60-3.

10. Koch, "Retribution," 60, 62-4, 65, 73.

11. Ibid., 58, 73.

12. John Barton, *Understanding Old Testament Ethics* (Louisville: Westminster/John Knox Press, 2003), 40-43.

13. Ibid., 6-8.

14. Moshe Weinfeld, *Social Justice in Ancient Israel and in the Ancient Near East* (Jerusalem: The Magnes Press; Minneapolis: Fortress Press, 1995), 7-8, 35, 45-6.

15. Waldemar Janzen, *Old Testament Ethics* (Louisville: Westminster/John Knox Press, 1994), 177-8, 206.

16. Birch, *Justice*, 259, 269.

17. Barton, *Ethics*, 78-80.

18. Ibid., 94.

19. Weinfeld, *Social Justice*, 198-208.

Chapter 3

1. Barton, *Ethics*, 132-7.

2. James Glanz and Eric Lipton, *City in the Sky* (New York: Henry Holt and Company, 2003), 4-6, 33.

3. Ibid., 5-6.

4. In Forrest Church, ed., *Restoring Faith* (New York: Walker and Company, 2001), 53-4.

5. Jared Diamond, *Collapse* (New York: Viking, 2005), 13-14

Chapter 4

1. Jim Wallis, *God's Politics* (San Francisco: Harper San Francisco, 2005), 98-9, 163.

2. Fyodor Dostoyevsky, *The Brothers Karamazov*, trans. C. Garnett (New York: Random House, 1950), 283-92.

3. David Ray Griffin, *The New Pearl Harbor* (Northampton, Mass.: Olive Branch Press, 2004), 96, 99, 230, 231.

4. Mark Lewis Taylor, *Religion, Politics, and the Christian Right* (Minneapolis: Fortress Press, 2005), 17-9.

5. Joseph Kelly, *Responding to Evil* (Collegeville, Minn.: Liturgical Press, 2003), 6-7.

6. Gordon Graham, *Evil and Christian Ethics* (Cambridge: Cambridge University Press, 2001), 88-90, 94.

7. Ibid., 93, 96.

8. Susan, Neiman, *Evil in Modern Thought* (Princeton and Oxford: Princeton University Press, 2002), xiii, 8.

9. Ibid., xvi, 9.

10. Ibid., xii-xiv.

11. Ibid., xi, 8-9.

12. Ibid., xvi.

13. Brueggemann, *Theology*, 73-6, 376-7, 390-3; "Some Aspects of Theodicy in Old Testament Faith," *Perspectives in Religious Studies* 26 (1999):253-67.

14. Koch, "Retribution," 81-3.

15. David B. Hart, "Where Was God?" *The Christian Century* (January 10, 2006): 26-9.

16. Dan O. Via, "Romans," *Mercer Commentary on the Bible, Vol. 7, Acts and the Pauline Writings*, ed. Watson E. Mills and Richard F. Wilson (Macon, Ga: Mercer University Press, 1997), 105-7.

17. Paul Ricoeur, *The Symbolism of Evil*, trans. E. Buchanan (Boston: Beacon Press, 1969),

241, 243, 251, 257-8.

18. Rudolf Bultmann, "The Question of Wonder," *Faith and Understanding* I, trans. L. Smith (New York: Harper and Row, 1966), 247-55.

19. Brueggemann, *Theology*, 401-3.

Chapter 5

1. John Rawls, *Justice as Fairness*, ed. E. Kelly (Cambridge, Mass.: The Belknap Press, 2001), 14-5, 78-9, 180-1.

2. Ibid., 42-3, 50, 52, 57-61, 64, 72, 76, 78, 88, 123.

3. James M. Childs, *Greed* (Minneapolis: Fortress Press, 2000), 32-4)

4. Ibid., 52, 54; Harold Wells, *A Future for Socialism?* (Valley Forge, Penn.: Trinity Press International, 1996), 140.

5. Wells, *Socialism*, 140.

6. Childs, *Greed*, 37.

7. Wells, *Socialism*, 77, 141.

8. Ibid., 141.

9. Childs, *Greed*, 6, 15-6.

10. Rawls, *Justice*, 58-9.

11. Elsa Tamez, *The Amnesty of Grace*, trans. S. Ringe (Nashville: Abingdon Press, 1993), 129.

12. Church, *Restoring Faith*; William H. Willimon, ed., *The Sunday after Tuesday* (Nashville: Abingdon, 2002).

13. See the sermon by Michael L. Budde of De Paul University in Willimon, ed., *The Sunday after Tuesday*.

14. Jean Elshtain, *Just War against Terror* (New York: Basic Books, 2003), 3, 6, 9-10, 12, 52-6, 74, 77, 93-4. Elshtain generally represents the position

of other well-known American scholars whose joint statement was released to the world press in February, 2002, under the title "What We're Fighting For—A Letter from America." This is reprinted in the book cited above, 182-207.

15. In Church, *Restoring Faith*, 87-90.

16. Sissela Bok, *Lying* (New York: Vintage Books, 1999), 108.

17. Rudolf Bultmann, *Theology of the New Testament* I, trans. K. Grobel (New York: Scribner, 1951), 15.

18. Flannery O'Connor, *Mystery and Manners* (New York: Farrar, Straus and Giroux, 1969), 112.

19. William Styron, *Set This House On Fire* (New York: The New American Library, Signet Books, 1960), 16-19.

20. Paul Ricoeur, *The Rule of Metaphor*, trans. R. Czerny (Toronto: University of Toronto Press, 1984), 44, 48, 98, 231, 299; *Interpretation Theory* (Fort Worth: Texas Christian University Press, 1976), 47, 49-50.

21. Ricoeur, *Theory*, 37, 50, 68; *Metaphor*, 229-30, 249, 290-1, 298-9.

Chapter 7

1. Rebecca Todd Peters, *In Search of the Good Life* (New York: Continuum, 2004), 201.

2. Michael Lerner, *The Left Hand of God* (New York: Harper San Francisco, 2006), 306-7.

3. Paul Krugman, The Daily Progress, (11/8/05), A, 10-11. *Washington Post News Service*, The Daily Progress (11/4/05): A, 1, 11.

4. Lerner, *Left Hand*, 307; Krugman, *Daily*.

5. I am dependent here on Jerry Mander, "Facing the Rising Tide," *The Case against the Global Economy*, ed. Jerry Mander and Edward Goldsmith (San Francisco:

Sierra Club Books, 1996), 4-5; David C. Korten, "The Mythic Victory of Market Capitalism," *Case Against*, 184-5; Jerry Mander, "The Rules of Corporate Behavior," *Case Against*, 309-10, 314-6; Kathryn Tanner, *Economy of Grace* (Minneapolis: Fortress Press, 2005), 34-9; Peters, *Good Life*, 36, 39, 48-50; Marie Cocco, "Inequality in a New Gilded Age," *The Daily Progress* (8/30/06): A, 10.

6. Kevin Phillips, *American Theocracy* (New York: Viking, 2006), 281-2

7. Cocco, "Inequality," A, 10; Clive Crook, "The Height of Inequality," *The Atlantic* (September, 2006): 36-7.

8. Cocco, "Inequality," A, 10.

9. Phillips, *Theocracy*, 385.

10. Associated Press, *The Daily Progress* (2/23/06): B, 1.

11. Associated Press, *The Daily Progress* (4/23/06): B, 1.

12. Jim Wallis, *God's Politics*, 222-3.

13. Associated Press, *The Daily Progress* (11/10/05): B, 1-2.

14. *New York Times* (11/13/05): Sect 3, 1, 4.

15. *New York Times* (12/11/05): Sect 4, 11.

16. Paul Krugman, "A New Age of Anxiety in Business," *The Daily Progress* (11/29/05): A, 8, 9.

17. Bill Moyers, "A Time for Heresy," Address at Wake Forest Divinity School (3/14/06): 2.

18. *The Christian Century* (August 8, 2006): 5.

19. Jon Gertner, "What Is a Living Wage," *New York Times Magazine* (1/5/06): 41-2, 62.

20. Ibid., 40, 72.

21. Ibid., 43-4, 62, 68, 72.

22. Ibid., 45, 62, 68.

23. Paul Krugman, "The Tax-Cut Con," *New York Times Magazine* (9/14/03): 54-62.

24. Hendrik Hertzberg, "War and Antiwar," *New Yorker* (September 5, 2005): 49.

25. Associated Press, *The Daily Progress* (6/9/06): C, 3.

26. Krugman, "The Tax Cut Con," 56-60; Associated Press, *The Daily Progress* (2/2/06): B, 1; (2/7/06): A, 8.

27. Krugman, "Tax Cut Con," 56-60.

28. Ibid., 56.

29. "Breaking the Code," *New York Times Magazine* (1/16/05): 34-9.

30. Both of these come from Bill McKibben, "The Christian Paradox," *Harpers* (August, 2005): 36.

31. Krugman, "Tax-Cut Con," 62.

32. Harry Kiely, "Privatizing Social Security," *Sojourner's Magazine* (March, 2005): 7.

33. Roger Lowenstein, "A Question of Numbers," *New York Times Magazine* (1/16/05): 42.

34. Ibid., 72.

35. Kiely, "Privatizing," 7.

36. Lowenstein, "Numbers," 72.

37. Ibid., 42, 78.

38. See the May, 2006, letter from the National Committee to Preserve Social Security and Medicare.

39. Phillips, *Theocracy*, 268, 319-20, 325, 334-5.

40. Ibid., 313, 327-8.

41. Ibid., 280-1, 327, 338.

42. Ibid., 329.

43. The *New York Times* (8/25/06): A, 21; C, 1, 4.

44. Hendrik Hertzberg, "Mired," *New Yorker* (August 22, 2005): 22.

45. Tim Flannery, *The Weather Makers* (New York: Atlantic Monthly Press, 2005), 3, 5-6, 28-9, 31, 79, 307.

46. Ibid., 285-7, 299.

47. Ibid., 222-4, 299.

48. Ibid., 225, 230.

49. Ibid., 232-4.

50. Ibid., 235.

51. Bruce Barcoff, "Changing the Rules," *New York Times Magazine* (4/4/04): 39-40, 44, 66, 76.

52. Philip Gordon, "The End of the Bush Revolution," *Foreign Affairs*, vol. 85, no. 4 (July/August, 2006): 83.

53. Washington Post News Service, *The Daily Progress* (12/21/05): A, 1, 6.

54. Hertzberg, "Mired," 21; New York Times News Service, *The Daily Progress* (9/30/05): A, 6.

55. Taylor, *Christian Right*, 58.

56. Jimmy Carter, *Our Endangered Values* (New York: Simon and Schuster, 2005), 74-5.

57. Taylor, *Christian Right*, ix, 1-2.

58. *Politics*, 142.

59. Taylor, *Christian Right*, 2.

60. *Left Hand*, 8.

61. Cal Thomas, *The Daily Progress* (2/15/06): A, 10.

62. Noah Feldman, "Who Can Check the President," *New York Times Magazine* (1/8/06): 54, 57.

63. Taylor, *Christian Right*, 68.

64. John W. Whitehead, *The Daily Progress* (2/26/06): B, 6.

65. Stuart Taylor, Jr., "The Man Who Would Be King," The *Atlantic* (April, 2006): 26.

66. *New York Times* (1/15/06): Sect. 4, 11; (6/28/06); A 16.

67. *New York Times* (7/16/06): Sect. 4, 11.

68. *The Daily Progress* (12/25/05): B, 6, 8.

69. Ibid.

70. *The Daily Progress* (5/31/06): A, 1,14; (6/18/06): B, 6, 8.

71. *Sojourners Magazine* (December, 2005): 40; John Perkins, *Confessions of an Economic Hit Man* (San Francisco: Berrett-Koehler, Inc.), 221; *The Daily Progress* (3/2/06): B, 2; (3/8/06): A, 8; Associated Press, *The Daily Progress* (6/16/06): C, l.

72. The material on this subject is from James Bamford, "Big Brother Is Listening," *The Atlantic* (April 2006): 65-6, 68, 70.

73. Associated Press, *The Daily Progress* (8/18/06): A, 1, 9.

Chapter 8

1. John Newhouse, *Imperial America* (New York: Alford A. Knopf, 2003), 8-21; Peter Singer, *The President of Good and Evil* (New York: Dutton, 2004), 131-6; John B. Judis, *The Folly of Empire* (New York: Scribner, 2004), 165-6.

2. Gary Dorrien, *Imperial Designs* (New York: Routledge, 2004), 80. Andrew J. Bacevich, *The New American Militarism* (Oxford: Oxford University Press, 2005), 11.

3. Vassilis K. Fouskas and Bülent Gokay, *The New American Imperialism* (Westport, Conn.: Praeger Security International, 2005), 4-5, 20-1. This position tends to be supported in Phillips, *Theocracy*.

4. Douglas John Hall, *God and Human Suffering* (Minneapolis: Augsburg, 1986), 42-46.

5. Gary Dorrien, *Imperial Designs*, 89.

6. David Rieff, "Blueprint for a Mess," *New York Times Magazine* (11/2/03): 28-33, 44, 58, 72, 77-8; John Burns, "There Is No Crash Course in Democracy," *New York Times* (12/14/03): Sect. 4, 1, 12; Douglas Jehl, "U.S. Certain that Iraq Had Illicit Arms," *New York Times* (3/6/04): A, 6: Peter Maass, "Professor Nagl's War," *New York Times Magazine* (1/11/04): 23-31, 38, 49, 56, 62; Max Boot, "The Lessons of a Quagmire," *New York Times* (11/16/04): Sect. 4, 13.

7. Associated Press, *The Daily Progress* (2/2/06): B, 1.

8. Dorrien, *Imperial*, 171.

9. Judis, *Empire*, 199.

10. Phillips, *Theocracy*, 350.

11. Fouskas and Gokay, *Imperialism*, 1; Robert Cooper, *The Breaking of Nations* (New York: Atlantic Monthly Press, 2003), 49.

12. Foreword by Peter Gowan to Fouskas and Gokay, *Imperialism*, ix.

13. Judis, *Empire*, 3-4, 13-17, 27, 30-6, 43.

14. Ibid., 38-40.

15. Ibid., 2, 51.

16. Ibid., 2, 51-2, 54-5, 59, 69.

17. Ibid., 5, 76-7, 99.

18. Ibid, 5, 76-7, 79-80, 92-3, 95-6, 104, 106, 114-5, 211.

19. Bacevich, *Militarism*, 175-9.

20. Ibid., 179-83.

21. Mark Danner, "Taking Stock of the Forever War," *New York Times Magazine* (9/11/05): 49.

22. Phillips, *Theocracy*, 70-1.

23. Judis, *Empire*, 172-4; Dorrien, *Imperial*, 2-4.

24. David Kay, "Iraq's Weapons of Mass Destruction," *Miller Center Report*, 20/1 (Spring/ Summer, 2004): 8; Peter Bergen, "This Terrorist Is Bad Enough on His Own," *New York Times* (6/26/04): A, 27; "Show Us the Proof," *New York Times* (6/6/04): A, 28.

25. Dorrien, *Imperial*, 183.

26. Associated Press, *The Daily Progress* (9/9/06): A, 1, 11.

27. Bacevich, *Militarism*, 201.

28. Dorrien, *Imperial*, 181; Judis, *Empire*, 184.

29. Phillips, *Theocracy*, 69.

30. Ibid., 75-6.

31. Eugene Peterson, "Pounding at an Elusive Target," *The Daily Progress* (8/14/06): A, 10.

32. Associated Press, *The Daily Progress* (9/19/06): A, 10.

33. Dorrien, *Imperial*, 1-2, 14-7, 75, 77,122.

34. Ibid., 27, 38-43.

35. Ibid., 68, 126, 130-1, 137-8, 170.

36. Ibid., 6, 75-8.

37. Michael Ignatieff, "Why Are We in Iraq," *New York Times Magazine* (9/7/03): 38, 40.

38. *New York Times Magazine* (3/14/04; 5/2/04; 6/27/04; 6/26/05).

39. Dorrien, *Imperial*, 255.

40. Judis, *Empire*, 195.

41. Bacevich, *Militarism*, 123-4, 126-8, 141.

42. Ibid., 145.

43. Ibid., 132; Phillips, *Theocracy*, 95-6.

44. Bacevich, *Militarism*, 146.

45. Philip Gordon," The End of the Bush Revolution," *Foreign Affairs*, 85/4 (July/August, 2006): 75-6, 81.

46. Fareed Zakaria, "Why We Don't Get No Respect." *Newsweek* (July 10, 2006): 49.

47. Ibid.

48. Ibid.; Gordon, "End," 76, 79.

49. Gordon, "End," 85-6.

50. Bacevich, *Militarism*, x, 1-2.

51. Ibid., 15, 17.

52. Eland, *Empire*, 25.

53. Fouskas and Gokay, *Imperialism*, 71.

54. Bacevich, *Militarism*, 18, 20-1, 23.

55. Ibid., 147.

56. Phillips, *Theocracy*, 85-6; Fouskas and Gokay, *Imperialism*, 22-3, 72, 150-1, 154, 156, 159.

57. Robert D. Kaplan, "How We Would Fight China," *The Atlantic* (June, 2005): 49-50, 58, 60.

58. Ibid., 54, 58, 60.

59. John Hall in *The Daily Progress* (12/8/05): A, 8; Jane Mayer, "Outsourcing Torture," *New Yorker* (February 14 and 21, 2005): 106-8.

60. Associated Press, *The Daily Progress* (4/27/06): B, l.

61. Hall, *The Daily Progress* (12/8/05): A, 8; Associated Press, *The Daily Progress* (12/6/05): A, 8; Mayer, "Torture," 106.

62. Mayer, "Torture," 106.

63. Ibid., 112, 114; Andrew Sullivan, "Atrocities in Plain Sight," *New York Times Book Review* (1/23/05): 8; *New York Times* (7/12/06): A, 18.

64. Ibid.

65. Chuck Gutenson, "Losing Our Souls." *Sojourners Magazine* (January, 2006): 8.

66. Susan Sontag, "Regarding the Torture of Others," *New York Times Magazine* (5/23/04): 24-9.

67. Michael Ignatieff, "Mirage in the Desert," *New York Times Magazine* (6/27/04): 14.

68. Marie Cocco, *The Daily Progress* (5/25/05): A, 10.

69. *New York Times* (8/25/04): A, 1,11.

70. Sullivan, "Atrocities," 9-10.

71. *New York Times* (7/24/05): Sect. l, 16; (7/12/06): A, 1, 18; *Washington Post* (10/15/05): A, 1, 11.

72. *New York Times* (7/12/06): A, 1, 18; (7/13/06): A, 1, 20; (7/13/06): A, 23.

73. Associated Press, *The Daily Progress* (9/29/06): B, 7; *New York Times* (9/28/06): A, 22.

74. Associated Press, *The Daily Progress* (9/29/06): B, 7.

75. Scott L. Silliman, "Troubling Questions in Interrogating Terrorists," *Duke Magazine* (September-October, 2004): 72.

76. Judis, *Empire*, 127-8.

77. *Economy*, ix.

78. *Imperialism*, 13.

79. Peters, *Good Life*, 41.

80. Ibid., 45-6.

81. Ibid., 54-5.

82. Ibid., 44-5, 47, 49-50.

83. Ibid., 46-8, 83.

84. Ibid., 88, 149.

85. Tony Clarke, "Mechanisms of Corporate Rule," *The Case against the Global Economy*, 300-1.

86. Ibid.

87. Jerry Mander, "Facing the Rising Tide," *The Case Against the Global Economy*, 13-14; Peters, *Good Life*, 47, 74, 144-5.

88. Mander, "Rising Tide," 13-14; Peters, *Good Life*, 44, 144-5.

89. John Perkins, *Confessions of an Economic Hit Man* (San Francisco: Bennett-Koehler Publishers,, 2004), 226-9.

90. Ibid., ix, xi-xiii, xvii, 15, 19.

91. Ibid.

92. Peters, *Good Life*, 194-5.

93. Bill Moyers, "A Time for Heresy," 4-5.

94. Perkins, *Hit Man*, xvi-xx, 203-6.

95. Jeffrey D. Sachs, *The End of Poverty* (New York: Penguin Books, 2005), 47-8, 281, 356-7.

96. Ibid., 357.

97. Ibid., 358.

98. Associated Press, *The Daily Progress* (9/27/06): A, 1, 11.

Chapter 9

1. Phillips, *Theocracy*, 300-1.

2. Ibid., ix, 268, 307.

3. Ibid., ix, 268, 271, 298-9, 306.

4. Flannery, *Weather*, 6, 97; Associated Press, *The Daily Progress* (9/14/06): C, 6.

5. Flannery, *Weather*, 88, 92-3, 95, 97-8, 169, 297.

6. Ibid., 170, 205-9.

7. Jared Diamond, *Collapse* (New York: Viking, 2005), 494-6.

8. Phillips, *Theocracy*, 271; 306, 311-14; 334; 336-40; 381.

9. *New York Times* (7/11/06): C, 1-2.

10. Phillips, *Theocracy*, 87-8; Peter Maass, "The Breaking Point," *New York Times Magazine* (8/12/05): 33-4.

11. Phillips, *Theocracy*, 328-9; *New York Times* (8/25/06): A, 21.

12. Phillips, *Theocracy*, 385.

13. James Fallows, "Countdown to a Meltdown," *The Atlantic* (July/August, 2005): 52-3, 57-8. 60-1, 63.

14. Robert O. Paxton, *The Anatomy of Fascism* (New York: Vintage Books, 2005), 13.

15. Ibid., 99-102; Mary Fulbrook, *A Concise History of Germany* (Cambridge: Cambridge University Press, 1994), 173-80; Larry Rasmussen, "The Steep Price of Grace," *Sojourners Magazine* (February, 2006): 18-20.

16. Rasmussen, "Steep Price," 18.

17. Paxton, *Fascism*, 40-2, 219-20; Laurence W. Britt, "Fascism Anyone?" *Free Inquiry* (Spring, 2003):1-5.

18. Elshtain, *Just War against Terror*, 3-6, 74-5, 93; Bernard Lewis, *The Crisis of Islam* (New York: The Modern Library, 2003), 26, 37-8.

19. James Fallows, "Declaring Victory," *The Atlantic* (September, 2006): 60.

20. John Rawls, *Justice as Fairness*, 6, 27, 42, 44, 46, 50, 87.

21. Ibid., 50, 57-61, 88.

22. Ibid., 44, 51-3, 136-40.

23. Ibid., 132-3.

24. Kathryn Tanner, *Economy of Grace*, 47-8, 62-3.

25. Ibid., 65, 66.

26. Ibid., 130-1.

27. *The Amnesty of Grace*, 130-1

28. Paul Tillich, *Systematic Theology*, vol. 1 (Chicago: University of Chicago Press, 1951), 302-3.

29. Ibid., 14-17; 93-4, 149-50.

30. Tanner, *Economy*, 62-3, 67, 73-6, 87, 89.

31. Ibid., 73-4, 76-8, 83, 130-1.

32. James M. Childs, Jr., *Greed* (Minneapolis: Fortress Press, 2000), 97-9, 103, 105.

33. Rebecca Todd Peters, *In Search of the Good Life*, 123, 139, 142, 198.

34. Ibid., 139; Mander, "Rising Tide," 18; Martin Khor, "Global Economy and the Third World," *The Case against the Global Economy*, 57; Tony Clarke, "Mechanisms of Corporate Rule," *The Case against the Global Economy*, 307-8.

35. Peters, *The Good Life*, 164; Mander, "Rising Tide," 18; James Goldsmith, "The Winners and Losers," *The Case against the Global Economy*, 178.

36. Childs, *Greed*, 10.

37. Mander, "Rising Tide," 18.

38. Herman E. Daly, "Sustainable Growth? No Thank You," *The Case against the Global Economy*, 192-3.

39. Daly, "Sustainable Growth?" 193-5.

40. Peter Singer, *One World* (New Haven: Yale University Press, 2004), 92, 94-5, 112.

41. Fouskas and Gokay, *The New American Imperialism*, 130-1.

42. Eland, *The Empire Has No Clothes*, 230, 238-9, 242-5.

43. Ibid., 230-3, 237, 244, 247, 250.

44. Ibid., 222, 241-4.

45. Bacevich, *Militarism*, 2-3, 17, 208-10, 213.

46. Ibid., 16-7, 214-5.

47. Robert Cooper, *The Breaking of Nations*, 3-4, 7-9, 22, 28, 45-6.

48. Ibid., 5, 16, 26-8, 32-3, 50, 70-2, 171.

49. Michael Ignatiff, "Why Are We in Iraq?" *New York Times Magazine* (9/7/03): 85.

50. Flannery, *Weather Makers*, 6, 166, 168, 267-8, 271, 279-80, 290-4, 298-9.

51. Singer, *One World*, 50.

52. Flannery, *Weather Makers*, 293-4.

53. Diamond, *Collapse*, 483-5.

54. Gregg Easterbrook, "Some Convenient Truths," The *Atlantic* (September, 2006): 29-30.

55. Flannery, *Weather Makers*, 302-17.

56. *One World*, 194.

57. *Economic Hit Man*, 221-2.

58. *The Good Life*, 203-7.

59. Cooper, *Breaking of Nations*, 163.